Praise for Within These Woods

"Within These Woods delivers an intimate and knowledgeable perspective on the flora and fauna of the Minnesota forest. It transports us from the page and into the wild. That transforms our worldview. When you really get to know something it is impossible to be ambivalent about its destruction."
-Anton Treuer, author of *Everything You Wanted to Know About Indians But Were Afraid to Ask*

"Goodwin's essays and drawings aren't just a walk through nature; rather, they each strive to establish the relationship between creatures and humans... Though I am a country boy, familiar with many of the animals described, each essay taught me something entirely new thanks to Goodwin's detailed observations and clear, sincere writing."
-Aaron J. Brown, Host *of The Great Northern Radio Show* (KAXE), and author of *Overburden: Modern Life on the Iron Range*

"While reveling in the complex relationships found in the ecosystem around us, Goodwin explores difficult questions about stewardship, spirituality and sustainability that he says can only be answered by examining our own personal connection with nature." -Bemidji State University

"The book is a thematic collection of Goodwin's poems, essays and artwork meant to provide Goodwin's answer to the broad question of how he, ⸻ ember of a globally interconnecte in the world. On his path to that ⸻ ⸮gance of evolution and the interco ⸮gs."
-Andy Bartlett

Other titles from Riverfeet Press

THIS SIDE OF A WILDERNESS: A Novel (2013)
- Daniel J. Rice

ECOLOGICAL IDENTITY: Finding Your Place in a Biological World (2016) - Timothy Goodwin

TEACHERS IN THE FOREST (2016) - Barry Babcock

ROAD TO PONEMAH: The Teachings of Larry Stillday (2016) - Michael Meuers

A FIELD GUIDE TO LOSING YOUR FRIENDS (2017)
- Tyler Dunning

AWAKE IN THE WORLD (2017): A Riverfeet Press Anthology

ONE-SENTENCE JOURNAL (winner of the 2018 Montana Book Award and the 2019 High Plains Book Award) - Chris La Tray

WILDLAND WILDFIRES: and where the wildlife go (2018)
- Randie Adams

I SEE MANY THINGS: Ninisidawenemaag, Book I (2019)
- Erika Bailey-Johnson

AWAKE IN THE WORLD, V.II (2019): A Riverfeet Press Anthology

FAMILIAR WATERS (2020) - David Stuver

BURNT TREE FORK: A Novel (2020) - J.C. Bonnell

REGARDING WILLINGNESS (2020) - Tom Harpole

LIFE LIST: POEMS (2020) - Marc Beaudin

THE UNPEOPLED SEASON: Ten Year Anniversary Edition (2021) - Daniel J. Rice

KAYAK CATE (coming 2021) Cate Belleveau

WITHIN THESE WOODS

A collection of nature essays with original illustrations by the author

Timothy Goodwin

Riverfeet Press

Riverfeet Press
Livingston, MT
www.riverfeetpress.com

WITHIN THESE WOODS
A collection of essays with original illustrations by the author
Second Edition
Timothy Goodwin
Non-fiction: Nature/Essays
ISBN-13: 978-1736089422
LCCN: 2015939101

Edited by Lotti Writing Services & Tracy Goodwin
All illustrations by the author
Typesetting & interior design by Daniel J. Rice
Cover background by Katerina Kreker/Shutterstock

Contents

WITHIN THESE WOODS
(Second Edition)

Timothy Goodwin

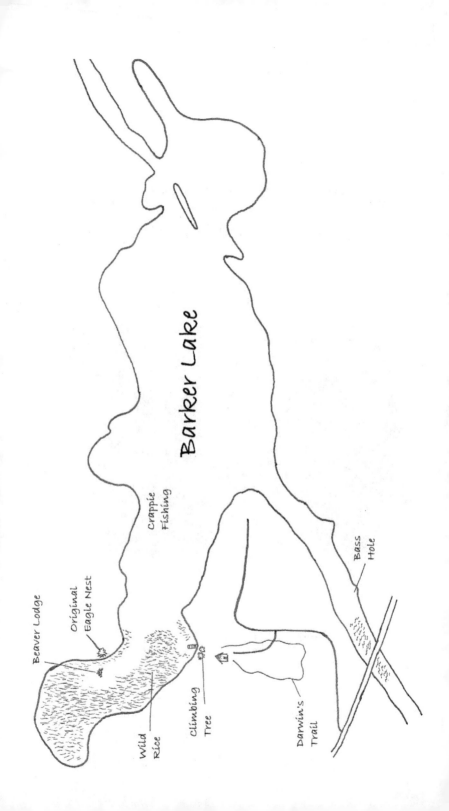

There are two things to be discovered in any forest: you and the forest. –Douglas Wood

Introduction

I see the world through the eyes of a biologist. I see more than trees, flowers and animals. Wandering and wondering through these woods, I see the connections between those organisms and also ponder my connection with them. This book is not only about the species inhabiting the northern woods of Wisconsin and the Great Lakes region, it is also an exploration of the connections between those species and ultimately my own ecological identity.

The log-sided family cabin within these Northwoods was built in the early 1980s. Before that, I recall spending weekends here camping in an old canvas tent in a flat open area down close to the lake, under the cover of large white pine trees. The ground under the trees was covered with pine needles, and the primary plant cover was a fine-bladed fescue grass, a little taller than mid-shin in height, but bent over, providing a tall but manicured look. The campsite included a well with a hand pump, a table, a fire pit, many mosquitoes, a primitive, one-hole outhouse, and rain storms. I remember many rainy weekends before we finished building the cabin. I also remember the smell of hot, dry wind blowing through the trees and across the dusty, brown pine needles among the fescue grass—a distinct odor that rushes back through my olfactory senses whenever I'm in the Northwoods in the summer. I still like that smell.

I was twelve when we began construction. My dad, my brother, Chris, and I were the main builders, but we relied heavily on the help of many of our friends. Dad and Chris completed the initial phase of construction during a week when I was not there, so from my perspective we went very quickly from a tree-filled woods with a campsite to the beginning of a cabin. The first sign of construction I saw was a twenty-by-forty-foot platform floor atop twelve telephone poles, with the canvas tent now perched on what would later become the main floor of the cabin. The site chosen for the cabin is up the hill a couple hundred feet from the original campsite. Because of the slope of the hill, the end of the platform on the lake side is eight feet off the ground.

The resulting cabin that grew atop that platform, almost magically from the perspective of my twelve-year-old eyes, was a modest structure. The main floor has an open floor plan housing the living room, centered around a wood-burning stove, an eating area with a picnic-style table made by Dad, and a kitchen area big enough for one cook, maybe two if they don't mind literally rubbing elbows. The back third of the main floor has a small bedroom, a bathroom with a shower stall, and a small storage closet. Above these rooms is a loft with two twin beds. At the center beam the loft ceiling is easily tall enough to stand under, but the roof angles steeply from the center beam down to the floor on each side, so that when in a loft bed it is best to sit up carefully to avoid smacking one's forehead on a support beam. Originally, the open space under the cabin between the telephone poles was a storage area. No matter how much cross-bracing we added to the telephone poles and joists underneath, you could feel the cabin rock back and forth slightly if you were lying in bed in the loft when someone walked across the main floor. This simple design provided all the space we needed when the family was just Dad, Mom, Chris and I.

Since the initial construction, Chris and I have added spouses and five grandchildren to the family, so the cabin has grown as well. A finished, walkout basement is now the foundation instead of the original, swaying telephone poles. This project added living space equal to the size of the main floor, including a second bedroom and another bathroom with shower stall. Storage needs are now met with a twenty-six by forty-foot garage, housing thirty years of accumulated boats, tools and toys. The most recent project is a two-person bunk house Dad constructed from maple logs from these woods.

The cabin sits on six acres along the shore of Barker Lake, which is not much more than a wide spot on the East Fork of the Chippewa River running through the edge of the Chequamegon National Forest. This portion of Wisconsin's Sawyer County is what is known as an interlobate moraine, a region between two intersecting lobes of glaciers from the Pleistocene Ice Age. The Pleistocene began some two million years ago, with glaciers eventually covering the entire Great Lakes region, extending into what are now the plains of the Dakotas and the entire northeast portion of North America. This last glacial period concluded with the melting and receding of the glaciers twenty-two to twelve thousand years ago. Where the cabin sits, the Wisconsin glacier left a thick layer of glacial debris—sand, rocks, soil, and large boulders—in its wake. Once the glaciers receded, plant life began to spread throughout the area. The most recent shift in plant life happened within the last hundred years after loggers cleared away most of the white and red pines. Aspen trees came first, followed by the maples, oaks, and basswoods that currently dominate the landscape. Pine, spruce, and fir trees are also part of the ecosystem.

I like to watch and hear the woods come alive in the early morning, usually before sunrise, while reading with a cup of coffee on the screened porch. We added this nine-by-twenty foot screened porch to the lake side of the cabin in the mid-nineties to replace the original deck, which still inspires laughter when we recollect how little we knew when we built it compared to how much we have learned since. If not enjoying morning coffee on the deck, I like to walk the driveway and nearby road or quietly paddle the perimeter of the little lake as the day comes alive. During these moments I realize that I am not a mere observer, but a member of the same ecosystem—sharing the same space, oxygen, radiant energy from the sun, and 3.5 billion years of evolutionary history. The bacteria, birds and humans share the same genetic building blocks—just reorganized, modified and mutated—creating a tangled bush of related species sharing the biosphere. During these moments of evolutionary clarity, I also realize that we do not own these woods. They own us.

Over the years, I have become more cognizant of the variety of life springing up from the forest floor. I glimpse birds darting between the leaves, calling to one another, often warning others of my presence. I identify some by sight, others by sound. For me, knowing the names of the birds, the trees that make up this canopy and the flowers that bloom throughout the spring and summer brings them from the background to the forefront. This increases my awareness of their uniqueness and their connectedness to the ecosystem of these woods.

When I was young, Dad took us for walks in the woods. Because we were kids, Chris and I complained about the walking biology lessons. How foolish we were. I now understand that knowing the names—or better yet, understanding the *stories*—of the species around us means understanding the interrelatedness of the life throughout the forest. Knowing particular names helps me connect with the particular spirit of that organism, and each spirit helps me connect to the whole and understand myself within it. I have tried, and failed, to memorize all of these names. It took me a long time to realize that memorizing the names was not how I would acquire this understanding. Instead, I have to dig in one species at a time, and discover its beauty by telling its story and understanding its natural history. Doing this work leads to a better understanding of these species; I learn about their evolutionary history, their role in this ecosystem, and more about what it means to have an ecological identity. It is through writing stories and poetry about them and also creating illustrations that I develop my understanding. Each of the species that follow in this book is presented with my original illustrations. Additionally, the uncredited poems that begin many of these essays are written by me as a means of exploring those species. By telling the stories of these species, and how they connect to those who have lived within these woods—the Ojibwe, immigrants who came later, and most recently, me and my family—I hope to pass on the same gift to my readers that my father passed on to me.

In little tunnels
Safe from danger above
Below the snow
Peromyscus rules
A place in which we do not go
A world all to themselves until
Our machines and trails interrupt and crush

Deer Mouse

Peromyscus maniculatus

Let's be honest about it. Can you think of the deer mouse, sometimes called the white-footed mouse, as anything but a pest? When they invade our space, who among us does not set a trap? More disturbing than finding a mouse might be finding only evidence—food half-chewed and droppings left behind. What all had it touched in that cabinet or pantry? Is anything safe from their "filthy" little feet?

Getting past such prejudice, I must acknowledge the tremendous success and survival of these little animals mice, even as they navigate their perilous world with so many predators and people out to get them.

I am awed by the deer mouse's evolutionary adaptations to survive so well in such harsh conditions, but in reality, every species faces equally difficult challenges and is equally well-adapted for the world in which it evolved. That is the beauty of evolution and why it fascinates me as I continue to explore the woods surrounding the cabin. It is a system with endless complexities and connections, yet operating on surprisingly simple rules of competition, adaptation, and survival. Despite perturbations great and small, from comet impacts that wiped out dinosaurs 65 million years ago, to subtle shifts in weather patterns that may eliminate some species, the system continues to self-correct and adjust. But can this system survive repeated disturbances?

Reflecting on my callous attitude toward the mouse's attempt at survival by invading my pantry, I think about our history of westward expansion into the "pantries" of others such as wolves, coyotes, or even indigenous peoples. We really are not much different than the mouse.

Philosopher and ecologist Arne Naess created a field of ecology called "Deep Ecology." His view was one of advocacy for the inherent worth of living beings regardless of their utility to human needs. A core belief is that the biosphere as a whole should be respected and all life within that biosphere has certain inalienable rights to live and flourish. This is not to say that no creature should ever kill another, because the sustainability of an ecosystem relies on the fact that organisms kill and consume one another. Wolves eat deer; foxes eat mice, and so on. Some would even kill Arne Naess if given the chance.

In my gut these core beliefs of deep ecology feel good. Not only does every species have a right to survive, but also because of the interconnectedness of all species, our survival is ultimately linked to the survival of all the other species with which we share this biosphere. These core beliefs shift our thinking from an anthropocentric environmentalism to a philosophical foundation that the functioning of the ecosystem, including humans, should be understood holistically and not as separate parts. But how would that play out? How would operating on these foundations change our behavior? Would this cabin, for which I have such affinity, be allowed to exist? Where is the line between existing, while utilizing the natural world to make a place for ourselves, and exploitation? Wherever that line is, I suspect we crossed it long ago as a society. We have the same inalienable rights to live and flourish as the next species, but I cannot deny our weed status, and I can imagine the earth as a giant shaggy dog, shaking violently to rid itself of fleas, even though we are doing what comes naturally to all species—adapting to and using natural resources to fulfill our needs. It is, I suppose, a matter of scale.

In the end, here we are, wrestling with our past, preparing for our future, and living in the present, trying to find our proper roles in this complex biosphere.

To waste, to destroy our natural resources, to skin and exhaust the land instead of using it so as to increase its usefulness, will result in undermining in the days of our children the very prosperity which we ought by right to hand down to them amplified and developed.

–Theodore Roosevelt

White-Tailed Deer

Odocoileus virginianus

Each spring, female deer usually give birth to twin
fawns. For the first few weeks, these delicate her-
bivores hide in the tall grasses or underbrush while
the mother forages nearby and returns to nurse them.
The fawn is a master at hiding and will stay perfectly
still even if a person walks very close to its bed. In

such a case, the mother will sprint away, flashing the underside of her tail as a warning to other deer in the area. When all is clear, she will return and continue foraging and nursing. After a few weeks, the fawns will begin to forage with their mom and their range will expand. Male fawns will usually stay with her for one year, while the females often stay for two.

These large mammals, second only to the black bear in average size in these woods, are the sprinters and high jumpers of the Northwoods forest. The experience I have of them is first seeing them quietly moving and browsing, and then watching them pause as they detect me with their noses, which have up to five times the olfactory receptors as does a bloodhound. Then they bolt off into the woods, easily leaping over fallen trees, darting off and melting into the underbrush.

As the fawns grow into adulthood, the males produce a rack of antlers. Each year the males produce a bigger and bigger set of antlers made of bone. As the males grow larger each season, they put more energy into producing a bigger and bigger rack. These antlers are then used by the males to spar with other males and dominate the females within their territories. A male deer's goal is to mate with as many females as possible, spreading his genes as widely as possible within the population. This is his sole contribution to the parenting of the offspring. At the end of each mating season in the fall, the male drops his antlers. The rodents in the ecosystem have come to rely upon these shed antlers. They chew on them both for the calcium and to sharpen and keep their teeth the right length. Antlers are rarely found on the forest floor. In 2013, the estimated deer population in Sawyer County was twenty-four thousand deer. If we assume that the bucks make up only twenty-five percent of the population, due to more bucks being harvested during hunting season, this would mean six thousand bucks dropping two antlers each season. There must be a lot of rodents chewing up these antlers.

Recently a single, young deer adopted the cabin for a season, no doubt attracted to our deer feeder. Once while walking on a trail near the cabin, my dad felt a nudge on his elbow from behind. There stood this young deer, as if asking for more food. He proceeded to feed out of a coffee can of corn held out to him by my dad. The yearling appeared to be in good health, so illness could not account for his brazenness. Later that same summer, I watched my youngest daughter and my nephew stand still, hands reaching out with corn. Slowly, the deer approached and eventually licked up all the food from their palms. We did not see the deer beyond that one season. We do not know the reason for his bravery, but it was probably his undoing during the hunting season that fall.

Deer hunting is now a necessity in these woods and all of North America populated by white-tailed deer. The deer population has grown incredibly during the last century as humans have nearly eliminated its primary predator, the wolf, and at the same time greatly increased the food sources for the deer with agricultural and landscape plantings. In most of the country, the only predators of deer are human hunters and cars. In many places, especially where deer hunting is not safe, such as suburban areas, deer routinely exceed the carrying capacity of the ecosystem. As the deer population becomes increasingly stressed and approaches mass starvation, they venture further into neighborhoods searching for food, decimating landscaping plants in yards and getting hit by cars. Every prey species needs a predator to keep the herd strong by culling out the old, the weak, and the sick and simply to keep the numbers in check.

In the woods around the cabin, the wolf population is growing, as it is in other parts of the United States and Canada. Coyotes and even the occasional bear will also prey upon deer. But the primary predator in these woods is still humans. In many ways, this is a seamless continuation of our history with the deer. The deer was always a staple food for the indigenous peoples throughout North America. However, in the early 1900s, the deer population was nearly elimi-nated by unregulated hunting. Hunting regulations and limits were eventually enacted and the deer pop-ulation rebounded—in many places, it has rebounded too much.

We continually try to manage other species, but our efforts often result in unintended consequences. We eliminate the predator of a species because it com-petes with our interests, but in so doing the popula-tion of the prey species becomes unstable. Now as the wolf population has grown in northern Wisconsin, a new conflict arises from hunters viewing the wolf as competition for the deer. Indeed we have created a sort of "love triangle" between deer, wolves and humans. If history is any indication, we will come out on top, at least in the short term. But history also tells us that we do not have a strong enough understanding of the intricate interactions between all the species to truly manage them. We must therefore tread as lightly as possible, for we do not even know with which step we will change an ecosystem.

"Only a mountain has lived long enough to listen objectively to the howl of a wolf."

—Aldo Leopold

Timber Wolf

Canis lupus

To the Ojibwe, the wolf is sacred. To many, the wolves are brothers, teachers, and guides to this world and the spirit world. While this is not my cultural background, I fully appreciate this connection. To many non-natives, the wolf has become sacred as a symbol of wilderness.

The timber wolf, or gray wolf as they are also called, was once native to much of North America and Eurasia.

This species of wolf shares a common ancestor with the domestic dog. These two subspecies diverged from one another about fifteen thousand years ago in Europe. Like the domestic dog, the wolf is a social animal, living in packs of up to ten individuals in which only the dominant alpha pair mate. Each year the alpha pair will have three to five pups and the entire pack will help care for them. The wolf has evolved sophisticated social behaviors allowing it to successfully hunt large prey such as deer, moose, and caribou—though it is only deer that share this ecosystem with the wolf. Large predators like these require large amounts of space to be able to get enough prey to support their high caloric needs. A wolf pack's territory may cover twenty to eighty square miles.

The conversion of much of the middle part of the North American continent from prairie and woodland to farmland caused conflict between the wolf and homesteaders. This predator was the last hurdle to clear in the taming of the American west, so the U.S. government offered a bounty on wolves. The raising of livestock and large predators such as the wolf simply do not mix. Once we realized, about fifty years ago, that this now endangered predator was a necessary component to keeping the white-tailed deer and other prey species in check, wolves were placed on the federally protected list.

As recently as 1980, the estimated population of Wisconsin wolves was twenty-five individuals, but because of federal protection, the wolf population has begun to increase in numbers again in the northern United States. The wolf was removed from the state endangered species list in 2004 and the federal list in 2012. The estimated population in Wisconsin in 2013 was around seven hundred individuals. As the population has recovered, limited wolf hunting has been allowed in Wisconsin and neighboring Minnesota. In 1999, the Wisconsin Department of Natural Resources created a wolf management plan including a goal of a sustained Wisconsin population of 350 animals. I frankly do not understand the desire to hunt a top predator like the wolf. It is not for the meat, to be sure. In the end, I doubt that the wolf needs managing.

The question then is how to share our home with our brother the wolf. Indeed, there are dangerous interactions when two top predators, such as wolves and humans, occupy the same locations. For the most part, however, wolves stay clear of humans, though they will occasionally venture onto farms and take livestock and even family pets. Instead of managing the wolves as competition, we should view them as a necessary cost of sharing this habitat.

Though wolves are becoming more common in these woods, I have never seen a wolf in the wild, and part of me hopes never to see one. It is better for the wolf if I do not know from where they come or where they go.

Death is nature's way of making things continually interesting. Death is the possibility of change. Every individual gets its allotted lifespan, its chance to try something new on the world. But time is called and the molecules which make up leaf and limb, heart and eye are disassembled and redistributed to other tenants.

–Peter Steinhart

Short-Tailed Weasel

Mustela ermine

The weasel is a fascinating predator. Its prodigious hunting ability is necessary to support its high metabolism. Because of a body shape inefficiently designed for heat preservation, a weasel's rate of metabolism is a crucial adaptation for the cold climate of the Northwoods. The general rule in ecology, called Bergmann's rule after German biologist Carl Bergmann, is that the further north, the larger the average body size. The counterpart to this rule is Allen's rule; put forth by Joel Asaph Allen, it states that the further north, the less surface area an animal will have to prevent body heat loss. This usually equates to shorter limbs and ears. While the body type of the weasel might fit Allen's rule, with its long, narrow, cylindrical body, short ears and short legs, it does not fit with Bergmann's rule, weighing in at only two to five ounces.

Maybe it is because of its strictly carnivorous diet and adeptness at hunting that the weasel's reputation has been besmirched in children's stories much like that of the wolf. These skilled hunters can take prey as large as a rabbit and will hunt every animal smaller than that—mostly small mammals such as voles and mice, but also frogs and insects as well. Historically we do not approve of such ferocious predators. This is of course ironic and hypocritical as the majority of people in the United States are themselves predators. But still, we created the mythology of the big bad wolf and the sneaky weasel. Fortunately, I believe this prejudice is softening, at least for the wolf, though I suspect most people are widely unfamiliar with the weasel except as a derisive term for someone they do not trust.

The short-tailed weasel probably would be described as big, bad, and sneaky by a mouse from the Northwoods. The weasel, because of its inefficient body type, spends much time in the subnivean air space below the snow, taking advantage of burrows and tunnels created by the smaller rodents' winter activities. The weasel freely moves about in this space, taking any prey it can find. What may be a fortunate day for a predator may well not be a fortunate day for the prey. But this is as it should be. One day the weasel will have its fortune and survive for another day by ingesting and utilizing the matter and energy found in the mouse. The next day a mouse may evade the predator, which will then fall prey to a larger predator, or simply starve to death, leaving the matter and energy stored in its body to be used by scavengers and decomposers. These organisms will return that matter and energy to the soil, to be used by the primary producers in the ecosystem. It is only through the lens of human morality do we root for one species over another.

The weasel, because of its size, is susceptible to predation as well, primarily by hawks. Camouflage is the main defense strategy for the weasel. During the summer months, the weasel sports a brown coat that blends in quite nicely with the dried leaves on the forest floor. During the winter months the brown coat is shed and replaced with pure white fur to match the snow cover. However, at all times the short-tailed weasel has a very ingenious additional defense strategy: diversion. The tip of the short-tailed weasel's tail is dark black. When the all-white weasel is moving across the snow-covered forest floor, instead of trying to move with complete stealth—which simply is not possible against a predator such as a hawk or owl—the weasel deliberately gives away the position of the tip of its tail. The movement of the black tip is what the bird of prey sees first. The bird's point of attack is the easy-to-see tip of the tail instead of the weasel's body. The weasel is much more maneuverable than the airborne predator, and by the time the bird has regrouped and gathered enough altitude to attempt another attack, the weasel has often found a suitable hiding place.

I guess this is a very *sneaky* strategy, though I prefer to admire the cleverness of design on the part of the weasel.

The predator swoops and dives
Scanning ahead and below
For signs of unsuspecting prey
Until he folds his wings
Dropping through the branches
Seizing its next meal
Today the hawk is fortunate
While the grosbeak's fate is sealed
But tomorrow,
Tomorrow, fortunes may change
Sealing the hawk's fate.

Cooper's Hawk

Accipiter cooperii

The first time I saw a Cooper's hawk was when I was a young teen, off on my own walking through the woods around the cabin. Before then, I had always considered hawks to be large birds only seen perched high above a roadside ditch or soaring over an open field, scanning the ground for prey. Deep in the dense woods of the aspen and maple forest was not where I expected to see a bird of prey.

It was a fleeting look at best. I was not even sure what I had seen. I knew it was a hawk because of its shape, talons, and beak, but I did not know there were hawks the size of a pigeon or maybe a crow at best. It flashed overhead, dodging and darting between trunks of trees, over branches, and crashing through the maple leaves. This was not a bird relying on stealth as it moved through the forest. For all I knew, this bird did not know how to leisurely fly through the forest. I was shocked to see a bird of prey in among the mid-level trees and brush of the forest instead of soaring silently high overhead. I chased, but within moments I knew there was no hope of keeping up with this aerobat. That was one of the first times I consciously replayed the image of a bird in my mind to recall the specific features for later identification. After this sighting, I headed back to the cabin and consulted the *Peterson Field Guide to Birds of Eastern and Central North America*.

I cannot say with certainty this was a Cooper's hawk. It could have also been a sharp-shinned hawk, as their markings and behaviors are similar. While the female Cooper's hawk is the size of a crow, the male Cooper's hawk is smaller—not much larger than a mourning dove or American robin—about the same size as the female sharp-shinned. I had either just witnessed a male Cooper's hawk or a female sharp-shinned. Like many hawks, the male is significantly smaller than the female. This is fairly unique in the animal kingdom. Sexual dimorphism usually favors the male of the species with a larger, more powerful physical presence. This is most often the case in mammals in which the male wins the right to mating one or multiple females by challenging and warding off other males of the species. Mountain gorillas and lions are classic examples. The males of a species such as these find their genetic success by mating with as many females as possible, spreading their genes across as many offspring as possible, as opposed to species that exhibit more monogamous trends, like many birds do, in which the key to genetic success is helping to ensure the survival of your offspring by aiding in their rearing.

In the case of the Cooper's hawk, this story of mate selection has an added element of danger and intrigue. Female Cooper's hawks specialize in eating medium-sized birds such as American robins or mourning doves—birds about the size of a male Cooper's hawk. Therefore, the males tend to be quite submissive to the females and reticent in approach until hearing a reassuring call from the females giving her approval for mating. After mating, the male is the primary nest builder and provider of food to the female and the chicks during the ninety days of growth before they fledge. This is either a devoted father and partner, or simply a male living in fear.

These hawks are some of the bird-world's most adept fliers. As I observed, they do not flit their way through the forest, but tear through the branches and brush at full speed. Aggressive flying is a necessity when hunting birds which are, themselves, quite maneuverable in the cover of branches, brush and deadfall. This is a dangerous lifestyle. In one study of Cooper's hawk skeletons, nearly one-quarter had healed fractures in their chest bones.

Once prey is captured, the Cooper's hawk makes the final kill by repeatedly squeezing the prey with its talons, slowly suffocating it, much like a constrictor snake slowly tightens its grip on prey. Unlike other birds of prey, they do not use their sharp beak as a killing weapon; instead, they hold the prey away from their body until it is dead. This is an adaptation necessary for a predator that is taking prey nearly as large as itself. In some instances, Cooper's hawks have been known to actually drown their prey, holding it under water until it stops moving.

Cooper's hawks are another example of a species that has benefited from the conversion of habitat into human civilization. Where people go, tend to go songbirds, mourning doves and pigeons all following easy food sources such as bird feeders. This provides Cooper's hawks with plentiful prey, easier to catch in the open airspace of suburban back yards and cityscapes than among the protection of a dense maple-basswood forest understory. After that first encounter with a Cooper's hawk, I do not recall seeing one again until a few years later. I was hiking woods in Southern Minnesota with classmates and a professor for a vertebrate biology class. With an overblown sense of pride for my accomplishment, I spotted the bird some distance off, recognizing it as a Cooper's hawk, though honestly, it very well could have been a sharp-shinned.

Since that second sighting, it seems I regularly see these birds. I do not know if their numbers have increased, maybe due to more open space and back-yard bird feeders luring in easy prey, or because I know what to look for and so notice them more. Once one knows what they are looking for, it is easier to find. However, the thrill of that first discovery is an irre-placeable experience. I think that is my lure to teach-ing. I cannot experience discovering something for the first time again, but I can now help others have that experience, which if you ask any teacher, witnessing that moment of discovery by the student when he or she finally "gets it" is the reason we teach. But as much as we try to replicate the real world in the classroom, nothing can beat the discovery a boy makes through a close encounter with an animal in the woods. Those discoveries and learning experiences last a lifetime.

Drip Drip Drip
Sap flows from the tap
Gallons of the sticky sap
Boiled down
To sweet syrup
And sugar

Sugar Maple

Acer saccharum

The wisdom of the forest is in the trees. Wisdom, or Nibwaakaawin in the Ojibwe language, is one of the seven teachings or Seven Grandfathers. For the Ojibwe, this means that cherishing knowledge is knowing Wisdom. Wisdom is given by the Creator to be used for the good of the people. The longevity, life cycle and succession from one species of tree to another makes trees the keeper of the wisdom of a forest ecosystem.

Sugar maples are the predominant tree species surrounding the cabin. They provide a gold and orange backdrop to the lake country in the fall. The largest can reach sixty feet or more. During even the sunniest summer days, the broad leaves provide a dense green canopy that blankets all the plant species below. Each fall, maple seeds helicopter to the forest floor. While most of the seeds do not successfully "plant," numerous offspring still emerge every spring, but only the strongest are able to pass on their genes. A maple must survive up to thirty snowy winters with regular sub-zero temperatures before reaching sufficient maturity to produce its massive amount of seeds.

I like an Native American story about the relationship between the sugar maple (Axsinaminshi) and the Northwoods birds for its telling of symbiotic relationships in the woods. Grubs and beetles burrowed beneath Axsinaminshi's bark, causing it to itch intensely. Despite his many limbs, Axsinaminshi could not find relief from the torment. In desperation, he called to the squirrels, porcupines, and beavers for help, but they offered only sympathy. Next, Axsinaminshi turned to the songbirds for assistance, but they too offered only sympathy. Then the woodpecker, appeared saying he could help. He brought his cousins, the flicker, and the downy woodpecker, and together they picked every pest from Axsinaminshi's bark. Relieved, he thanked them for their aid, and the woodpecker and his cousins thanked the sugar maple for the tasty grub and beetle meals.

Years later, a distressed woodpecker called his fellow woodland creatures, seeking help as he was dying of thirst due to a long drought. Axsinaminshi encouraged the woodpecker to come to the sugar maple's trunk and drill some holes. The woodpecker flew down and pecked away at the trunk, making holes that filled with sap. He drank joyfully, saved from his thirst. Perhaps the Native People learned to collect the sap from watching the woodpecker drill into the tree.

I imagine a wooded area two hundred years ago similar to that which currently surrounds the cabin. It is known as the "sugar bush" because the maples have protruding taps with sap dripping into birch bark baskets. Traditionally, each Ojibwe family group had their own sugar bush with a small supply lodge and boiling lodge in the middle. Sap was boiled to thick syrup, strained, replaced in the kettles, and heated slowly. When thickened to the proper consistency, it was transferred to a "granulating trough" and worked with a paddle and bare hands until in the form of granulated sugar. Sometimes, the syrup was poured into little cones, birch bark dishes, or even a duck's upper mandible to make hard candy—a favorite confection for children.

Beyond syrup, of course, the maple tree is an important source for construction projects requiring a hard, dense wood. Parallel strands of cellulose fibers in the wood are held together with lignin. The closer together the fibers and the longer the chains of these fibers are, the more dense and strong the wood is. Wood from maples has tight, straight lines of cellulose, making it denser and stronger than the wood of fast-growing trees such as aspen or pine. This makes maple a prime choice for furniture or wood flooring. The cabin is built from pine because it is light, strong enough, and fast growing, making it more of a renewable resource, but we availed ourselves of maple for the original deck railing.

I clearly recall making the railing on the original deck. We first gathered maple poles eight to fifteen feet in length and three to four inches in diameter and then removed all the limbs. The bark was stripped by pulling a drawknife along the entire length of each pole. The larger diameter poles became the vertical posts while the smaller diameter poles constituted the top railing and also were placed in a crisscross pattern between each vertical pole. The resulting railing was decorative but not terribly sturdy, thanks to the difficulty of connecting together round poles with our limited woodworking skills and tools. Plus it served almost no purpose as an enclosure to the deck that was at least ten feet above the ground. The maple, though dense, hard, and useful for such indoor applications as furniture and flooring, is not resistant to rot, making our choice a poor one for a railing exposed to the elements. Further testament, I suppose, to the do-it-yourself and learn-as-you-go attitude with which we approached the cabin construction. However, pieces of that original maple crop can still be found inside the cabin in some pieces of furniture, handrails, and poles. Protected from the moisture, fungus and bacteria decomposers prevalent under the shade of the canopy of trees, this indoor use of the maple is just right, and has been a long-lasting part of the cabin construction.

The family that uses this cabin consists of three generations, but is close-knit, and includes just eleven individuals: my Mom and Dad, my brother, his wife and three boys, me, my wife, and our two girls. Each of us brings something different to the family and cabin when sharing this space. And even though quiet solitude in the woods energizes and rejuvenates me, the cabin, absent the commotion of family cooking, playing, and working together, is just an empty building. The cabin full of family at ease with each other and this place is like those select maple logs. If not cared for and nurtured, the relationships can decay and sour, but in these woods, and within this cabin that necessitates collaboration, the fibers making up the family relationships remain straight, true and strong. This is the wisdom of the trees.

At the start of spring I open a trench
in the ground. I put into it
the winter's accumulation of paper,
pages I do not want to read
again, useless words, fragments,
errors. And I put into it
the contents of the outhouse:
light of the sun, growth of the ground,
finished with one of their journeys.
to the sky, to the wind, then,
and to the faithful trees, I confess
my sins: that I have not been happy
enough, considering my good luck;
have listened to too much noise;
have been inattentive to wonders;
have lusted after praise.
and then upon the gathered refuse
of mind and body, I close the trench.
folding shut against the dark,
the deathless earth. Beneath that seal
the old escapes into the new.

—Wendell Berry ("A Purification")

Spring Beauty

Claytonia virginica

Spring Beauty marks the arrival of spring, blooming as the snow melts in late April or early May. It is the first wildflower to appear, emerging in small clumps through decaying ground cover where the sun has warmed the thawing ground. It is an unassuming little plant, unnoticed most of the year, except for the month it creates a little white and pink bloom. A collection of prickly pine needles, crunchy maple leaves, and small pieces of branches obscures it at first, but the spring beauty works through the detritus of last year's growth. I suppose this flower knows what we all must eventually learn: that we carry "detritus" with us—poor decisions and lapses in judgment that have been detrimental to self or, worse yet, damaging to relationships with loved ones. But we can work our way through the decaying muck and even turn it to our advantage as we grow and mature.

As the little white flower reaches upward, the decomposers and detritivores work their way downward. Though too slow and microscopic to see with the naked eye, these bacteria and fungi extract energy from the detritus on the ground and, in the process, release nitrogen, nucleic acids, potassium and phosphorous—the building blocks of future generations of growth. These organisms are the true recyclers of the ecosystem. Plants re-use the molecules they release, forming the foundation of the local food chain.

The Spring Beauty is a perennial herb that grows about six inches tall and eight inches wide. The potato-like tuber embedded in its root system stores chains of sugar molecules as starch for the plant's growth, although humans can use it as a delectable treat when it is boiled or roasted.

One never knows what is hidden below such ephemeral beauties of the world. It causes me to wonder how many ephemeral ideas or individuals I may have overlooked, not allowing enough time to see their potential and let them flourish. How many ideas from students during my career as a high school teacher did I not provide enough time for? How many meet a similar fate now that I am a college professor? How many times was I too short with members of my family? It takes a commitment of time, energy, and thought to simply stop, listen and hear.

If I sit quietly with eyes closed, I can almost hear the sounds of forest life using energy to create order in the form of growing and recycling, all starting from the brilliant chaos of the sun's energy. The tuber of the Spring Beauty is the real treasure of this plant, the result of months of daily solar energy transformed through photosynthesis. The packets of photonic energy from the sun strike the chlorophyll molecules in the leaf, dislodging electrons and transferring them to another molecule. As these electrons click into place around carbon atoms, surrounding molecules convert the sun's light energy into chemical energy as sugars. As the roots grow and tunnel through the soil, they become intertwined with fungal filamentous mycorrhizae, which aid in water absorption. One at a time, water molecules work their way up the stem, defying gravity due to the seemingly magic attraction of surface tension between the water molecules and the sides of the plant's vascular tissue. Sticking together like little magnets, as one is drawn up the stem of the plant it pulls an endless chain of water molecules, connecting together the water vapor in the air around the leaf, the cells in the leaf, the stem of the plant and the water in the soil around the roots. The hydrogen atoms in the water molecules provide an ongoing source of electrons to replace the ones previously dislodged by the light photons striking the leaf, allowing photosynthesis to keep occurring in the leaf.

Normally, crunching leaves beneath my feet obscure my imagining of these sounds of forest life, both micro and macro. Sighting the Spring Beauty causes me to pause, quiet my own intrusive sounds, and listen. What these woods tell me is that learning comes at a cost. The price is mistakes. As a father, spouse, and teacher, what can I do so that those around me can have a safe place to learn from their mistakes, an opportunity to reflect on the detritus of their own growth?

A thing is right when it tends to preserve the integrity, stability and beauty of the biotic community. It is wrong when it tends otherwise.

—Aldo Leopold

Wood Anemone

Anemone quinquefolia

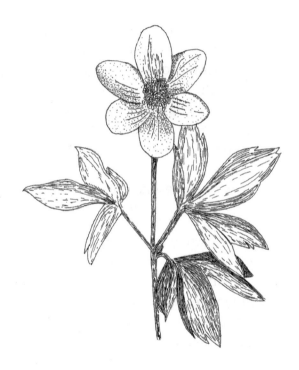

The *Anemone* is the introvert of the spring flowers. It reminds me of a close friend of mine who does not say much. But after taking time to carefully consider his thoughts, he shares his ideas which are always highly valued by those around him. I have rarely witnessed this friend leaving a gathering. He simply slips out, and some-time later, others notice his absence.

Like my friend, the *Anemone* appears briefly, presents itself to the forest floor, quickly bears fruit, and then disappears when the spring sunlight no longer reaches the forest floor after the maples fill in the canopy with new leaves. The blooming wood anemones signify that the ground is warming and fully-leaved trees of summer are soon to follow.

When the *Anemone* is in bloom, it is easy to miss. It is a simple flower: the petal-like sepals are white to pinkish-purple in groups of five, though sometimes four or six, perched at the top of a four-to-eight inch stem. It thrives at a trail's edge and other areas where the spring's sunlight reaches. It uses horizontal rootstocks spread across the surface of the ground for support. The flower is diurnal, enticing visits from daytime pollinators such as bees and bee-like flies, and then closing at night to preserve precious water.

I often confuse this flower with Spring Beauty (*Claytonia virginiana*) as both are demure, early-spring ephemerals. The difference is in the leaves. The *Anemone* has three long-stemmed leaves, each with three to five deeply toothed leaflets branching in a whorled configuration, while *Claytonia* has simple, long, skinny, grass-like leaves branching off the stem partway between the ground and terminal flower.

Despite its diminutive stature, I imagine the spirit of the wood anemone as one of quiet confidence. Maybe this is why this tiny plant has such cultural importance worldwide. The Chinese plant it on graves, calling it the "death flower," while the Persians believe that air blown across a field of *Anemone* becomes a poison for those unfortunate enough to be downwind. Greek mythology has the blooming red anemone signifying a restoration of the earth's fertility after Adonis' annual sojourn to the underworld.

For me, the passing of the wood anemone's flowering life stage marks the transition from spring to summer. Goodbyes must be difficult for the wood anemone and my friend alike. I do not know the reason, and doubt I ever will, but I suspect it centers on the concept of humility. Humility is another of the seven teachings from the Ojibwe, or Dadaadendiziwin in the Ojibwe language. You are equal to others, but not better, and always a sacred part of Creation. Maybe this is the common story the wood anemone and my friend share and the lesson to be learned from them.

We stand now where two roads diverge. But unlike the roads in Robert Frost's familiar poem, they are not equally fair. The road we have long been traveling is deceptively easy, a smooth superhighway on which we progress with great speed, but at its end lies disaster. The other fork of the road — the one less traveled — offers our last, our only chance to reach a destination that assures the preservation of the earth.

—Rachel Carson

Spring Peeper

Pseudacris crucifer

One knows the Spring Peeper's presence in early spring not by sight but instead by tiny choruses of peeps, one each second. When many call at the same time, it can sound like sleigh bells. These tiniest of the Northwoods amphibians, at ³/₄ to 1 ¼ inch long, are the first to call in the spring. They are easy to identify if you can find them by the distinctive, dark, X-shaped marking on their back contrasted with the light, gray-green color of their body. Hence their species name of *crucifer.*

Calling is the exclusive responsibility of the male. He sings his song from shrubs and trees rooted in or hanging over the water. He is near the water because the eggs he fertilizes, like those of all amphibians, must remain in fresh water. These eggs do not have the luxury of a waterproof shell or an "internal pond" like mammals, so if not laid in water they quickly dry out.

He is attempting to lure females, which generally prefer those males with louder and faster calls. Sexual selection by the females has caused the male to evolve faster and louder calls over generations, even though this trait exposes them to predators. Sexual selection often drives the evolution of the males in the opposite direction that nature would select. In other words, the very traits that might cause a female to find and choose a mate are often the same traits—such as bright feathers or loud mating calls—that need to be dulled in order to allow the prey species to hide from a predator. This contrast between what attracts the females to the males and traits that allow the males to hide from predators is a compromise between reproductive success and survival. These opposite pressures on the males to be seen and the females to remain hidden often result in sexual dimorphism (such as male cardinals being bright red while females are duller in color). It is a delicate dance indeed, but finding a mate is worth the risk.

Each individual frog's song adds to the chorus of the woods. Indeed, they might all sound the same to our human ears, but make no mistake, the females can tell the difference. If they could not, then the females would never actually locate an individual. They would be just as overwhelmed by the chorus as are we humans.

Some males do not sing, choosing instead to silently hide and wait. When the female comes to find the male producing the alluring call, the silent interloper intercepts her and steals his rival's chance at mating. This sneaky behavior is quite an evolutionary advancement. These males use the call of a nearby male to draw in the female, but if the call also draws in a predator, they can stay hidden.

The Latin word *crucifer*, which means "cross bearer," is an appropriate name for any amphibian, as the modern-day amphibians have a significant cross to bear. They are the metaphorical "canaries in the coal mine" for ecological concern. All amphibians spend most of their lives in water. They do not have gills like fish, but instead absorb oxygen through their skin, partly because they do not have the same need for consistent, abundant levels of oxygen that we warm-blooded animals have. When the temperature or oxygen level drops, frogs can simply slow down their metabolism. This adaptation, which has worked to their benefit for millions of years, is now quite dangerous. In addition to absorbing oxygen through their skin, they also absorb any chemicals in the water. Atrazine, a widely used pesticide, might be one of the worst. Research has found that this chemical can cause male frogs to turn into female frogs. Some research has also linked the absorption of these chemicals, in connection with a natural parasite, to alarming cases of disfigurement like extra or split limbs.

But incidents of disfigurement are not the primary signal of ecological trouble. The real alarm for scientists is simply silence. The reduction of amphibians, or worse, the extinction of species, indicates not only loss of crucial wetland habitat—habitat necessary for the cleansing of our water supply—but also the increased pollution of surviving wetland habitats. This is a worldwide concern. Once thought of as swamps and wasted space because they could not be used for growing crops or development, wetlands are now recognized as crucial natural water purifiers, protections against flooding, shoreline stabilizers, essential habitat for many species, and beautiful natural ecosystems.

In 1962, Rachel Carson changed the role of scientists and nature writers from the realm of researchers and thinkers to activists with her book *Silent Spring*. She was criticized for this role change. Many scientists who make this shift from researcher to activist are often still criticized. She was right, however, and her publication illuminated the impact of pesticides such as DDT and predicted a silent spring due to the lack of bird song. It also eventually resulted in the ban of DDT in the United States. This was not an easy fight, and corporations with a great deal of business on the line used considerable monetary and political resources to fight her efforts. But the movement she began not only saved birds such as the bald eagle and California condor but also gave birth to modern environmentalism.

Rachel Carson once said, "We still talk in terms of conquest...We still haven't become mature enough to think of ourselves as only a tiny part of a vast incredible universe." In reality, we are just as tiny and fragile as the frogs. Fifty-some years later, this mindset still eludes most of us.

Nature doesn't have a design problem. People do.

—William McDonough & Michael Braungart

Jack in the Pulpit

Arisaema triphyllum

Early spring wildflowers are always a welcomed sight at the cabin, especially along the path around the perimeter of our six acres, which was dubbed *Darwin's Trail* by my dad's biology teacher friends. It is a great place to go for an early morning spring walk with the dog to think and plan the day. Sunlight is brilliant through the leafless trees and each discovered wildflower poking its head out of the leaf litter is a treat. Along the trail, we have preserved the herbaceous woodland wildflowers and ferns that thrive in the heavy cover of the maple–basswood forest canopy that shades the forest floor during the summer months. Because of this, the woodland wildflowers primarily bloom before the trees and shrubs leaf out. One of the most unique of these is Jack in the pulpit.

This flower, which blooms in April and May, is like no other of the woodland wildflowers; while the leaves resemble the largest specimens of large-leafed trillium, that is where the resemblance ends. What makes this flowering plant unmistakable is the single flower atop a thick, green, rigid stem. The flower's long, brown, two-to-three inch tubular spadix (Jack) is tucked inside the protective envelope of a spathe (the pulpit) made from a single vase-like leaf, striped green and brown, which not only surrounds the spadix but also curves up and over the top like a hood.

Jack in the pulpit starts out as male for the first two years of its perennial life, but then will turn female and produces fruit and seeds. If stressed or shocked, the plant will turn back into a male. To the untrained eye, telling the difference between the male and female is difficult. The male flowers are somewhat smaller but the main distinction is a structural one. Male flowers have a small hole at the base of the spathe that allows pollinators an easy escape, hopefully after becoming loaded with pollen. The female flowers lack this hole, forcing the pollinator to move around the inside of the spathe searching for a way out, thereby increasing the chance of pollen from a male plant getting deposited on the spadix of the female plant.

At the end of the season, the female will produce a bright red, berry-like fruit clustered around the length of the spadix. The rest of the plant dies away, leaving only the bright berries, each carrying one to five seeds. These seeds germinate and form a tuber-like corm underground to give rise to a new plant. Each year a new set of leaves and flower will re-sprout from the underground corm, which contains a reserve of starches to fuel new plant growth.

The fruit and especially the wildflower are not edible, but the corm can be eaten if properly prepared by drying and roasting. The plant contains high levels of calcium oxalate crystals as well as other chemicals, giving the plant a strong, peppery taste. The sharp calcium oxalate crystals pierce the tongue and lips of the dining animal, allowing the other chemicals to enter its cells. This creates a strong and lasting burning sensation. Chewing tobacco companies have co-opted this strategy and put a sharp, fiberglass-like material into their products to aid the absorption of nicotine into the blood stream of the consumer. Drying the corm for at least six months removes the acrid, peppery taste and roasting it breaks down the calcium oxalate molecules so they no longer contain sharp points. Some indigenous peoples prepared the corm in this manner, and then ground it into a flour to make breads.

I am always amazed at our ability to find medicinal and dietary uses for plants, especially in cases where the first attempts at using or eating them must have produced undesirable effects. How might it have come to pass that someone would think about drying, storing and cooking the corm of the Jack in the pulpit, and then having the courage to give it another try after experiencing such bitterness the first time? As much as I am struck by the ingenuity of people to utilize plants in a variety of ways, I am even more awed by the variety of strategies for reproduction and survival that have evolved in those plants.

Which is preferable
A wood filled with sounds mysterious
Or empty silence and its rush?
Would you rather hear
Wind, frogs, trees and birds
Or thoughts demanding to be heard?

Cope's Gray Tree Frog

Hyla chrysoscelis

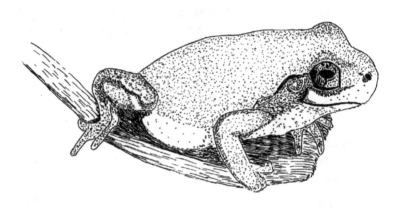

The call of the Cope's gray tree frog is the loudest sound in the evening woods. The male sings a sharp metallic trill during the breeding season from mid-May through June. All of the frogs combined create a chorus of song much like jungle sounds from a movie soundtrack. These little amphibians, at just over 1 to 2 ½ inches each, are responsible for a majority of the sounds in the nighttime woods.

Finding one of these frogs pressed up against the glass of a cabin window at night usually results in oohing and ahhing over their froggy cuteness. It comes to the window hunting for bugs, which are attracted to the cabin light spilling out into the surrounding blackness. An acrobatic hunter, the frog clings to the window with mucus-covered sticky pads until it leaps away to snatch a bug and then return back to the glass. It is not just the gluey mucous that allows the frog to stick to smooth surfaces like glass, but also the surface design of its toes. Its feet are made up of microscopic ridges and slits. When in contact and hanging on the surface, these ridges flatten out and increase the friction with the glass, causing the frog to stick. As the frog lifts up its foot, one ridge releases at a time. Simultaneously mucous is released and washes dust out of the channels between the ridges, cleaning its feet as it walks.

Identifying a Cope's as a "tree frog" is easy. It is gray to green, depending on the temperature, humidity, and current surroundings. Like some reptiles, its color can change in a manner of seconds. This is not because the frog can detect the color around it and camouflage itself, but is instead an indication of changing "moods" as a result of stimuli around the frog. Usually they are green with a black band behind the eye that extends down onto the front legs. The Cope's gray tree frog is difficult to distinguish from an Eastern gray tree frog, except by the call or by examining its chromosomes. The Eastern tree frog is a tetraploid, with four sets of chromosomes in each cell. The Cope's is a diploid (like me and you) with two sets in each cell, one from each parent.

The male calls for one purpose: to get the girl. Some males— like their spring peeper counterparts—remain silent, intercepting a female when she looks for the calling frog. The female produces up to two thousand eggs in batches of ten to fifty. The majority of the eggs never hatch, serving as food for fish and other aquatic animals instead. As a general rule, the lower on the food chain, the more offspring or eggs a species produces. Also, the less the parents tend to the offspring, the more eggs are produced as most of the eggs produced will not survive long enough to hatch. Those that do hatch, do so within a few days, and then take two months to metamorphose into adult frogs. Those few that reach adulthood retreat to the trees. I have not observed this journey and am not sure how long it would take a one-inch frog to climb thirty feet or higher up these trees. The frogs will continue filling the woods with their call, especially after evening rains, even when no longer attempting to attract a mate. It makes me wonder if they are singing just for the joy of it.

I find the woods filled with these sounds more comforting than when silent. I revel in the quiet sounds of a lively forest: early morning bird and frog song with a choral backdrop of light breeze through the trees. Some people find a quiet time of meditation peaceful and renewing. Frankly, I find it exhausting. Like many, I have tried practices such as prayer, meditation, and other means to empty my thoughts and let the world speak to me. But for me, those practices separate me from the natural world, and it is then that I feel alone and isolated. I am sure a skilled meditator or cleric would say I am missing the point, and I am sure they are right. But when surrounded by eerie silence, I hear too much. For me, silence by itself is an invitation to regrets: remembrance of loved ones wronged by bumbling actions, the sound of past conversations gone wrong, decisions made in haste, relationships fizzled away and opportunities squandered. This is probably natural for someone getting ready to send their own children off into adulthood. So I am always grateful for the jungle sounds of the little frog keeping my thoughts company and reminding me of the simple wonders of a life connected, the opportunities I have been provided by my parents and this place, which has been an instrumental part of informing, and continuing to inform, my ecological identity. Others might say I am hiding, but what better place to hide than within the chorus of the hardwood forest?

A solitary stem rises
From the leaf litter, supporting
Groups of three: leaves, sepals, and petals,
A product of springtime sun reaching
The floor of the deciduous forest

Two is a partnership—simple and intimate;
Four makes a team—providing safety in numbers,
    but requiring a leader
Three however, is a magic arrangement
Three can endure—just enough for a circle
Three provides support and friendship
As well as space for solitude.

Large-Leafed Trillium

Trillium grandiflorum

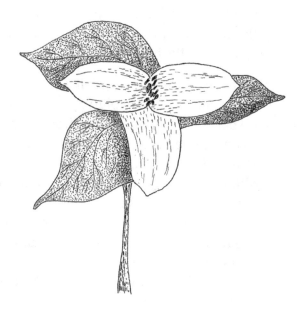

Trillium grandiflorum, or large-leafed trillium, consists of a single stem supporting three broad leaves, three sepals, and three white petals. This plant grows eight to fourteen inches tall and dominates the forest floor from late May through June. The plant rises each spring from a bulb deeply buried in the shaded, moist soil. Too much sun and this flower wilts and dies. If an area is clear-cut or even thinned, the prominent and abundant trillium will not survive.

The large flower, with its symmetrical three leaves framed by three long, narrow sepals, attracts pollinators. As it ages, the white flower develops prominent parallel veins that guide pollinators to the flower center in the way that landing strip lights guide a plane to a runway at night-time. These reddish veins give the flower a pinkish hue as it reaches the end of its life cycle and produces the fruit. The trillium fruit, appearing in July, is about one inch in length, angular shaped and green, red, or purple. Smaller seeds develop inside a fleshy covering.

The symbiotic relationship between ants and trillium is a wonderful example of co-evolution of two seemingly unconnected species. Ants collect and drag the fruit back to their nest, consuming the fleshy part and discarding the seeds untouched, thereby effectively planting them. Seeing a new trillium blossom from one of the newly planted seeds requires patience because it can take up to six years to produce a flower. Other forest creatures utilize this plant as well. The leaves are edible to deer and humans alike, and native tribes of the Great Lakes region used it to treat a number of ailments, including sore breasts, ear aches, rheumatism, eye swelling, and cramps.

My use for this plant is not nearly as tangible. I find a lesson in the power of groupings of three. As a teacher I have observed working groups of three to be the most productive. Groups of four or more can splinter into sub-groups. Partnerships are either very successful and productive or dysfunctional. There seems to be little middle ground. My closest friendships have always come in groups of three as well. As a young teen, I was somewhat lost in the larger world of high school; I got along with most everyone, but was not closely connected to anyone. I appeared to be happy and well adjusted, which maybe, compared to many, I was. Close enough to witness meaningful, comforting relationships but not quite close enough to touch is still a painful and lonely way to go through life. This social dynamic changed during a pivotal school trip during which I formed a bond with two friends that held for the remainder of my teenage and young adult years. We had a larger circle of friends but we could always return to the comfort of our trio. Within this trio, all ideas, insecurities, foibles, mistakes and successes were welcomed and celebrated.

This lesson on the value of these relationships came at a great cost. The eve of my senior year in high school is marked by the suicide of a classmate, a young man with a quiet and gentle soul. We had many classes together and often collaborated on schoolwork, played saxophone together in the band, and were always friendly toward one another. I do not think he ever found his trio. He truly was a young person hiding in plain sight in that large, suburban high school. Every now and then, something sparks memories of this event and I am thankful for the role my two friends played in helping me find my place.

"What day is it?" asked Pooh. "It's today," squeaked Piglet. "My favorite day," said Pooh.

—A. A. Milne

Red-Eyed Vireo

Vireo olivaceus

Most people probably cannot identify the red-eyed vireo by sight, even though they most likely have heard its call. Invariably it is the male we hear when he, like many of the songbirds, sings to attract a female to his territory. The vireo sports a bold face pattern, with a white eyebrow bordered in black and a ruby-red eye. The body is blue-gray, with contrasting olive-colored back and wings.

Except for its eye and white eyebrow, this bird blends in with the leaves of a tree.

No matter where the vireo goes, his song follows. If you have walked in the woods, or even in a neighborhood park, you are familiar with this bird. His call is so ever-present that it might be simply the "sound of the woods" to many people. The red-eyed vireo is the optimist of the woods, constantly and cheerfully emitting his short phrases: *sawee, sawitt, cheer-o-wit, cher-ee, chit-a-wit.* Each male has up to thirty different calls in his repertoire. Whether building his nest in the crotch between tree trunk and branch, foraging for caterpillars and aphids, or stuffing his mouth with berries to build up fat reserves before migrating as far as South America, he does not stop singing. On May 27, 1952, Louise de Kiriline Lawrence counted the songs from a single vireo at 22,197 songs, meaning the bird sang for 10 of the 14 hours of daylight.

Optimism seems to work for the vireo. This migratory bird has certainly found success in the world, with its range covering nearly all of North America and into South America during the winter, and even spreading to Europe. I have also found optimism to be a helpful tool. A few years ago, I made a conscious decision to purposefully approach all my students, my colleagues and the parents of my students with the assumption that when I am dealing with them they are "bringing their best."

I recognize that this approach is often naïve, meaning I am living in happy ignorant bliss like that "silly old bear" Pooh, and that in many cases, the person standing in front of me is not doing their best with their gifts. But if I do not accept this paradigm, what is the alternative? At the very least frustration and possibly even judgment and anger, which serve no one. Maybe on any given day, the best a student, colleague, or parent can do is simply to show up. Instead of greeting that effort (or lack thereof) with a negative reaction, what if I were to greet him or her the same way the vireo greets me every time I walk through the woods? What if we all took a lesson about optimism from the vireo? It is not about lowering one's expectations or standards, but about meeting others where they are in that moment, and then rising up from that point, together and in collaboration.

It is a century now since Darwin gave us the first glimpse of the origin of the species. We know now what was unknown to all the preceding caravan of generations: that men are only fellow voyagers with other creatures in the odyssey of evolution. This new knowledge should have given us, by this time, a sense of kinship with fellow creatures; a wish to live and let live; a sense of wonder over the magnitude and duration of the biotic enterprise.

—Aldo Leopold

Rose-Breasted Grosbeak

Pheucticus iudovicianus

In the early morning, the bright, cheery song of the rose-breasted grosbeak rings through the canopy of tall maples and the few remaining aspens. Bits of clear blue sky are visible through the leaves. The morning sunlight streams through gaps in the canopy and washes everything it illuminates with a golden hue. I look and look but cannot spot him. His call continues to haunt me, seemingly from all sides. Is he moving along with me as I walk, or is his voice echoing around me? I am sure that it is a grosbeak I hear and not a robin, though the songs are similar, with lengthy warbles that rise and fall. The grosbeak adds a short "cheep" at the end of his repeating pattern of cheery, clear warbles.

His nest and mate must be somewhere in the area. Grosbeaks are monogamous, though monogamy among songbirds has a more liberal definition than among humans. Most songbirds are considered socially monogamous and raise the chicks together, though they may mate with others. Therefore, the brood being raised by most pairs consists of many half siblings. This makes sense from an evolutionary standpoint in regard to genetic diversity, but does not have the same romantic ring to it as true monogamy does to our human sensibilities. The more the male can mate with a variety of females, or frankly the more the female can have half-siblings, the more genetic diversity in a population and the fewer instances of inbreeding. Many socially monogamous pairs will only remain together for the season and then find new pairs the next season. This is not a conscious plan or choice on the part of the birds. Simply put, the birds with the genes to be socially monogamous spread their genes among more offspring. Many of those offspring will inherit those genes and behaviors, thus perpetuating the behavior in the population—a simple, but very efficient, elegant, and effective strategy. This is an example of the wonder of evolution that strikes me as I walk these woods.

Each pair produces one or two broods per year, housed in a nest built of loosely-intertwined twigs and coarse plant material lined with fine twigs, rootlets, or hair. The male is primarily in charge of site selection, and the female is the primary nest builder. The result of their work is a cup-shaped nest, five to fifteen feet above the ground. The song of the grosbeak this morning comes from higher up than a probable nesting site would be. If he were foraging for food, he would not be up so high in the trees, since seeds, fruit, buds, a flower or two are all on or close to the ground.

Finally, through an opening, I see him sitting atop the tallest tree among the half-emerged spring leaves exploding from buds. A few days prior, the leaves were just in their infancy. A few days from now, I would not be able to spot him through the canopy of maple, aspen, and oak trees. He is perched well above the still-hidden nest site. Is he just singing for the joy of it? Maybe singing feels good to him just as singing a low, rumbling note feels good to me as it resonates in my chest. Researchers have begun to explore the idea that singing releases endorphins (the pleasure hormones) and oxytocin (the stress-reliever). Singing in a group might be meaningful because it begins with something so personal—a sound emanating from within, releasing pleasure hormones—but then combines with those of a chorus, creating a communal effect. Is our communal singing an evolutionary advancement to draw humans together in community? Could it have the same effect on avian brains as it does on humans?

This grosbeak is not trying to attract a mate. If he were, he would be crouching, spreading and drooping his wings, and spreading his elevated tail to show off his color and health. Or he would be singing and waving his body and head in an erratic dance. But he is not doing any of these things; he is stoically perched on the tallest tree, soaking the white part of his breast with a golden hue from the morning sun. Maybe the sense of kinship I feel toward this songbird is that he too might be simply enjoying a beautiful spring morning.

Sometimes what we are looking for is right there if we look high enough. I pause and wonder how much I have missed when I have not had the patience to keep looking. Patience is such a valuable virtue. A little patience can reveal the joy in nature, and the joy in nature can make us perch atop the highest spot, bathe in the glory of the rising day and make our own song heard just as this fellow is doing today. The odyssey of evolution is frenzied at times, but is afforded the luxury of eternity to conduct trial and error. I know that patience is not one of my virtues, but I do try to improve this skill. My virtue, I think, is knowing when and where to look for the lessons and I suspect that more time in the woods, staring up to the sky, searching for an elusive grosbeak is a good place to start.

Ah to be alive
on a mid-September morn
fording a stream
barefoot, pants rolled up,
holding boots, pack on,
sunshine, ice in the shallows,
northern rockies.

Rustle and shimmer of icy creek waters
stones turn underfoot, small and hard as toes
cold nose dripping
singing inside
creek music, heart music,
smell of sun on gravel.

I pledge allegiance

I pledge allegiance to the soil
of Turtle Island,
and to the beings who thereon dwell
one ecosystem
in diversity
under the sun
With joyful interpenetration for all.

  –For All, by Gary Snyder

Snapping Turtle

Chelydra serpentina

The common snapping turtle is Wisconsin's largest turtle. Barker Lake and the East Fork of the Chippewa River that feeds and drains it is ideal habitat for the snapping turtle. This species prefers densely weeded, slow-moving or still water with muddy bottoms rich in small fish, aquatic insects, frogs, and plants.

These turtles have a reputation as ferocious hunters and aggressive animals. In some regards this reputation is aptly earned. When out of the water, these animals will aggressively defend themselves, and they have the weaponry and armor to do so. They look tough. Their feet sport long, sharp claws with webbing between the toes, their carapace sports symmetrical ridges and points, and their muscular, thick tail looks like it came from an alligator. It is mostly show however, and if encountered on land they are not hunting. Turtles must eat in the water, because they need the aid of the water pressure to swallow their food. When in the water, it is a much better strategy to rely on stealth and escape instead of confrontation. Therefore, despite their prehistoric, dinosaur-like appearance, they are of virtually no threat to swimmers.

If one does encounter a snapping turtle out of the water it most likely will be a female because the main purpose for traveling over land is to lay eggs. Female snappers will travel up to half a mile or more on land looking for a suitable place to deposit her eggs. Around the cabin, the soil is plenty sandy, but in addition to sandy soil, the nest location requires enough sunlight to warm the eggs. Consequently, the most suitable location for nests is often the edges of gravel roads and roadside ditches.

Once a suitable nest site is found, the female will dig a hole in the sand with her back legs and deposit ten to one hundred leathery-shelled eggs, the size of a ping-pong ball, and then cover them with sand and leave them behind. There is not a particular breeding season for snappers and mating will happen throughout the year, though it most often occurs in the spring or fall. After 55 to 125 days of incubation, depending on the temperature and conditions, the eggs will hatch. The sex of the offspring is determined by the incubation temperature. Females result from warmer temperatures and males from cooler temperatures. The majority of the hatchlings do not survive. In fact, the majority of the eggs do not survive since they are unprotected from predation. If they do hatch, then the hatchlings must survive predators, cars, and dehydration as they leave the nest to find water on their own.

Overproduction of eggs or offspring is a common survival strategy. The general rule is that the less parental care taken in protecting the eggs or raising the offspring, the more fully developed the offspring are when hatched or born and the more there are of them. In fact, the ecosystem and the overall health of the turtle population would not be well-served if more turtles survived. This would deplete prey species and ultimately cause a population crash for the turtles when food sources and suitable habitat were exhausted. The overproduction of offspring is also the first rule of Darwin's theory of evolution by natural selection. A species will overproduce, thus leading to intraspecific competition. This leads, ultimately, to the population being made up of individuals with the adaptations best fit to that particular environment.

Those individual snappers that do survive can be very long-lived. Once they get large enough and are in a suitable, stable habitat, then their only predator is humans. Snapping turtles have been a popular choice for hunting. They can get quite large, with a carapace sixteen inches or more in diameter. A turtle of that size is quite thick as well, with considerable meat. Turtle soup was an early staple food for the Europeans who settled in North America. Despite heavy hunting pressures at different times, their population has always been stable—probably due to their reclusive behavior, heavy armor and longevity as individuals. In fact, there are reports of Wisconsin snapping turtles being captured with Civil War era Sharp's rifle bullets embedded in their carapaces.

It is not just the individuals that are long-lived. The species has remained unchanged for hundreds of thousands, maybe millions of years, and turtles as a group have remained largely unchanged since before the dinosaurs. I think it is because of their continuous presence throughout all of human evolution and history, coupled with their size, slow-moving nature, and somewhat prehistoric appearance that most cultures hold turtles in a place of wisdom, father-hood, or as a part of their creation stories. Stephen Hawking recounts a story at the beginning of his book, *A Brief History of Time*, about the turtle as the support for the earth:

> A well-known scientist (some say it was Bertrand Russell) once gave a public lecture on astronomy. He described how the earth orbits around the sun and how the sun, in turn, orbits around the center of a vast collection of stars called our galaxy. At the end of the lecture, a little old lady at the back of the room got up and said: "What you have told us is rubbish. The world is really a flat plate supported on the back of a giant tortoise." The scientist gave a superior smile before replying, "What is the tortoise standing on?" "You're very clever, young man, very clever," said the old lady. "But it's turtles all the way down!"

Oral stories from many of the Great Lakes indigenous peoples hold the turtle as a powerful symbol. Some creation stories do indeed speak of the turtle as the base upon which the first land formed. Many indigenous nations refer to North America as Turtle Island. In the oral tradition of the Ojibwe, Turtle Island is the land upon which they traveled westward to their home in the Great Lakes region, where they settled when they found the prophesied staple food of wild rice.

On a recent spring canoe trip from Barker Lake down the East Fork of the Chippewa River to the Chippewa Flowage, I saw a grand example of this species perched precariously on a large boulder at the edge of the water. From my viewing distance, it looked as if someone must have placed it on top of this boulder. The back side, which was out of my vision, must have been sloped enough for this massive turtle to pull itself up the smooth rock surface, because the three sides of the boulder I could see were nearly vertical. Before we could move any closer, it saw our approach and rocked its weight enough to fall off the side of the rock and enter the water with quite a splash.

My first encounter with snapping turtles is a much more distant memory. When I was five or six years old, someone delivered to my father a peanut butter jar filled with sand and a collection of turtle eggs. I do not know who found the eggs or why he would have disturbed the nest, but because my dad was a biology teacher, this person must have thought he would know what to do with them—beyond leaving them where they lay, which it was too late to do now.

I can remember watching them hatch as the baby turtles broke through the leathery shells with their beaks and front claws and the two-inch miniature turtles emerged from their artificial nest. I do not recall what happened to all of the turtles—whether they survived or not, were released, or ended up in classrooms somewhere. I do know that we kept one turtle and it spent the next twenty-five years in my father's biology classroom during the school year and in our house during the summer. The turtle had grown to a size of ten inches in diameter when it was finally released. I suspect that living in captivity with limited space kept this specimen smaller than she might have gotten if living in the open waters of Barker Lake; that, or my recent sighting was of a turtle of significant age and enough wisdom to know to get off the rock before we could get any closer. Ah, to be alive on a warm spring day, floating the river while pledging allegiance to one ecosystem, in diversity, under the sun. Swim far and deep, Grandfather Turtle.

The wild is a pathway to contemplation, learning, and wonder.

—Mitchell Thomashow

White-Throated Sparrow

Zonotrichia albicollis

"**P**oor Sam Peabody, Peabody, Peabody," the clear, jubilant call of the white-throated sparrow rings through the treetops. While other birds sing with similar volume, the white-throated sparrow sings with singular style. His is a long, drawn-out call that sounds (with some imagination) as if he is singing the song of some poor fellow, "Poor Sam Peabody, Peabody, Peabody." I hear the constant chitter-chatter of the evening songbirds as background music and continue on my way. But when the white-throated calls, I stop, isolate his call from all the other sounds, and take the time to listen to all he has to say. This was one of the first birds Dad taught me to recognize by its call, which makes it even more beautiful.

The white-throated sparrow's appearance is also distinctive, with a white chin, yellow forehead and black or brown and white stripes across his crown. I expect to find him foraging around, looking for buds yet to burst open with new leaf growth. Or maybe down on the ground, scratching through leaf litter hunting for a meal of seeds from herbaceous ground cover. I do not actually need to see him. Hearing the song alone will do. "Poor Sam Peabody, Peabody, Peabody."

Being able to label the birdsong is important, for it allows me to know who shares these woods. Knowing the song allows me to visualize what the bird is doing, where it is, and how it is surviving. This allows me to feel connected. The song of a bird such as the white-throated sparrow is paramount to its identity. Their song differentiates them from other species, and within their own kind, from one another. If I could not connect the unique song to the species, my understanding of its place in these woods would be incomplete. When I know a bird's song I can see all I need to with my ears.

It has been difficult to watch my dad lose much of his hearing during the past few years. When I hear a bird such as the white-throated, it pains me to know that he is not able to hear (and therefore "see") as many of the birds in these woods as he once could. This increases my desire to hear these birds, not just for myself but also for him, and then to pass that skill on to the next generation. Maybe, by continuing to hear these birds—and from hearing them, know them—we will have another reason to preserve them and their habitat.

"Poor, Sam Peabody, Peabody, Peabody," he sings again. Maybe there is a nest nearby, built by the female. It would be a simple, cup-shaped nest of coarse grasses on the ground, maybe resting along a forest edge in scrubby undergrowth. The female builds the nest and incubates the eggs, but the father helps care for the young for the entirety of their seven-to-ten-day youth. The rest of the world must appear to move very slowly for a creature that rushes through its life stages so quickly. Does the white-throated even notice me? I suspect not. I am as stationary to him as the large erratic boulders left by long-ago retreating glaciers are to me. I certainly notice him, and find irony in the fact that observing a creature with such a fast-paced life causes me to slow the pace of my life and pause on this morning walk.

"Poor Sam Peabody, Peabody, Peabody." The soaring song rings out yet again, stopping me in my tracks, slowing my heart and causing a catch in my breath. How can this little bird have such power? The song has a similar hold on Omakayas, the young Ojibwe protagonist in Louise Erdrich's *The Birchbark House*. Omakayas is one of the few survivors in her family after smallpox rips through her tribe. As she is recoiling from the realization that most of her family is lost, she hears the song of the white-throated sparrow "through the air like a shining needle, and [it] sewed up her broken heart." Omakayas is a truly heroic figure because she gleans strength to continue pressing forward from the world around her, never retreating into herself or giving in to grief and despair.

The clear tone of this bird connects me to the heroic people that first inhabited this region, living off and within these woods long before the voyageurs, settlers, and visitors coming north to visit for weekend getaways. My pause when I hear the white-throated's song is my way of thanking him for this lesson. When I hear "Poor Sam Peabody, Peabody, Peabody" piercing through all other sounds everything else disappears—for a brief moment anyway— and I realize what he might actually be saying is, "Live life, gratefully, gratefully, gratefully!"

The leaf stands upright
A green backdrop
To a flower, white and simple
Advertising the blood red root
Medicine
Toxin
Ceremony

Bloodroot

Sanguinaria canadensis

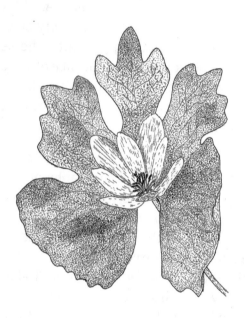

I like flowers that are easy to identify. Maybe that makes me a lazy naturalist. Maybe I am too distracted with the rest of life. Maybe I just do not have the wiring in my brain to be good at memorization. Maybe my attempts to memorize facts about the life in these woods have been a mistake. That was not my path to honoring them, their stories, and their spirit. So instead I focus on what I am good at: understanding the forces that connect the life within these woods. I wonder if we allow our children to do such things—to find their place and their passions. I worry that we are too focused on who they will be instead of who they are at the moment. A six-year-old is not a miniature adult waiting to be molded. She is and should be a six-year-old, with a six-year-old's emotions, body, and mind.

As a young father, I loved to read A.A. Milne's *Winnie the Pooh* books to my children. I'm pretty sure I enjoyed them more than they did. I appreciated the sensibilities portrayed in the book and the innocence of the characters. At the same time, Milne also captures this fleeting time in a child's life, one that seems to become more ephemeral with each generation.

When I was a child, I loved the national park programs about the plants, animals, and geography of a park, shows about animals like *Wild America* and *Wild Kingdom*, and the magazine *Ranger Rick*. These presentations, shows, and publications promoted the beauty and wonder of wildlife and natural habitats. A few years ago, I noticed a shift in the messages about nature aimed at children. Today's children hear repeatedly that this natural splendor is now endangered and it will be up to their generation to save it. That seems like an awfully heavy burden to put on the shoulders of a six-year-old. I wonder if this next generation even notices the weight. Or is this simply their reality? The world is endangered—period. That is simply the nature of nature. Just writing this saddens me nearly to the point of despair. At first I do not know what to do with this despair. I am initially paralyzed by it, but then the answer becomes obvious. This is what we can do: we can pass on the reverence for this place, these woods and this world, so the next generation can then do the same. This reverence and traditional, historical knowledge could be as much our legacy to the next generation as technological and scientific knowledge.

I fear that because of this new paradigm, our next generation of naturalists will not have the privilege of enjoying nature simply because they feel a connection and an attraction to the beauty of the natural world—labeled "biophilia" by E. O. Wilson. Being able to look at a plant or animal, name it, and talk a little about its adaptation with those sharing a walk in the woods brings me pleasure, just for the sake of knowing it. If it is an easy-to-identify flower like the bloodroot, then all the better. I fear that we are packaging connection to the natural world with also saving it, and therefore making it too overwhelming to be worth the effort. Everything rewarding does not have to be difficult does it?

Bloodroot is a perennial, preferring shaded, moist, rich woodlands. Full grown, it is about six to seven inches tall with a single leaf wrapped around the emerging flower. The round stem turns orange or red when mature and is topped with a single white flower made of eight to twelve petals protecting a bright yellow center. The root itself is a thick, tender, tuber containing a red juice that is an effective stain or dye.

While the bloodroot is toxic, it also has strong medicinal qualities when applied to skin ailments. Indigenous peoples throughout North America used it as medicine and extensively as paint and dye. European settlers discovered the medicinal qualities soon after their arrival, taking advantage of the flesh-destroying properties of the root juice by applying it to ringworm, warts, polyps and fungal growths. It is the same principle used, unfortunately, in treating cancer patients with chemotherapy. Sometimes healthy cells are necessary collateral damage when helping our body fight battles against certain diseases. It is, sadly, also the same principle our society seems to use in regard to the natural world. We view it as wonderful and splendid, until beneath its surface lies a resource necessary to continue a way of life predicated on unfettered growth—then it becomes collateral damage and the responsibility of the next generation to recover and restore.

Bloodroot has been integral to the health of humans for hundreds, maybe thousands, of years. It reminds me of a protective parent. The toxic qualities of the plant are a defense mechanism from predation. The leaf wraps around the flower, cradling it safely until the flower emerges, much like a parent cradles and protects a child, then gives her more and more freedom until she blossoms.

I remember my amazement while watching my oldest daughter show the first signs of her own personality. From me and my wife came this whole new person. I continue to be amazed as she develops, needing me less each step of the way as she discovers the things in life that give her joy, and also some that cause pain. Those things that bring pain are the most difficult to witness as a parent—watching mistakes, difficulties with relationships, errors in judgment. I want to block and prevent these from ever happening, but I also know they are important lessons for her to experience. Everyone must find their own way. Malcolm Margolin recounts this saying from a California Indian educator: "When you teach someone something, you've robbed the person of the experience of learning it. You need to be cautious before you take that experience away from someone else." Even armed with this wisdom, it is never easy to witness. Child psychologists, educators, and parents used to think of children as blank slates. I prefer the metaphor of an artist's canvas. It begins with a texture that is integral to the art form. Each experience contributes new colors and textures to the canvas, adding complexity to the picture as the individual incorporates these new elements into prior experiences and constructs meaning unique to them as individuals.

It is natural and feels right to be protective as long as possible as a parent, like the leaf protecting the flower. But it is also natural to be like the leaf by eventually opening up and allowing the flower to be exposed. My generation will pass on the mistakes we have made to the next and can only hope they have the resilience and skills to solve them. Perhaps Mother Earth and this great big biosphere within which we have evolved cradles and protects us and it is we, not Mother Earth, that are as fragile as that single flower contained within the leaf of the bloodroot. The optimist in me hopes that Mother Earth looks at us as the loving parent who watches her child make necessary mistakes. Ultimately, the earth will be fine with or without us, and hopefully our species will survive these teenage years of our technological development.

The male bird fills the woods
With his two-note call
"Spriiing-time"
An answer comes from not too far away
"Spriiing-time"
The same two words, but a whole tone lower
I know spring is here
Because the chickadee told me so

Black-Capped Chickadee

Poecile atricapillus

I share this morning's walk with a black-capped chicka-dee. The chickadee never seems to relax, reminding me of Templeton, the rat, from *Charlotte's Web*: always darting, searching and scanning for the next meal. When he finally stops moving, he calls out to announce the change in sea-son with a simple two-note "spriiing-time." The second note is a slightly lower tone and shorter in duration than the high-pitched, drawn out initial note. Simple, elegant, and true: springtime is here. A second chickadee answers from nearby, his notes a step down from the first, distinguishing himself for any listening females to hear.

But that is not all chickadees have to say. They are most well-known for their signature call, which can be imagined to be saying, "chickadee, dee, dee, dee." This quick call is common chatter throughout the continental United States, and earned them their name from the French settlers. The Ojibwe called it Che-ki-che-gua-na-sa, meaning "the bird that calls che-ki-che."

The most heard call of the chickadee, however, is one that most humans cannot even hear, but is crucial to so many other species with keener hearing than we humans possess. Using high-pitched alarm chatter, barely audible to our human ears but easily heard to all other birds, the chickadee serves as the sentinel in the treetops, warning all others of my presence on this spring morning. "Shhhh," I want to tell him. I mean him no harm, and if he keeps calling out his warning, I will never get to see the fox that lives in the den up at the top of the hill.

Though he seems intent on carrying out his cautionary duty, I do not know how I have injured or offended him. Black-capped chickadees have not suffered from human existence and settlement across the United States. These birds once were commonly found in and amongst the evergreens, white and red pine, white and black spruce, and balsam fir, but now these overly-energetic birds can be found wherever birdfeeders offer an easy and guaranteed year-round meal. These little birds require an abundance of food to get through the winter, and therefore are the prime visitors to Northwoods birdfeeders. They do not migrate south at the change of season and must keep active during the bitter cold of the Northwoods winter. A single bird needs to eat 150 sunflower seeds a day to survive in mild winter weather, and 250 seeds a day when the temperature drops below freezing. I imagine 250 sunflower seeds in my hand. Now I imagine the size of the stomach inside a five-inch bird; in my mind I cannot fit all of those seeds in. To propel energy around its body, the heart of a chickadee pumps 650 times a minute. Fortunately, it does not have to maintain that pace indefinitely. It does rest at night, when its body temperature drops to 68 degrees Fahrenheit to conserve energy. Without this drop, it would starve to death before morning. This is one species that has formed a strong mutualistic relationship with human settlement. We provide additional food, and they provide entertainment.

I imagine that when not spying on the progress of my walk, the chickadee gathers food for the hungry chicks back in the nest, for he is a devoted father. There are no birdfeeders or sunflower plants in the woods around the cabin, so he takes what he can find: insects, caterpillars, seeds, berries, spiders, even the fat from carrion. While his mate waits on the nest, his responsibility is to find enough food for the entire family. He must take this contribution seriously, because chickadees stay with their mates in long-term, monogamous relationships. She will incubate six to eight eggs for twelve to thirteen days, then care for them for another fifteen to sixteen days. The pair usually leaves the area entirely after three or four weeks, then returns to produce another clutch if the season permits.

I will continue my walk, enjoying the call of "spring-time," which is echoed by another male some distance away, with full knowledge that every animal within earshot now knows I am on my way. Every forest needs a chickadee.

A flash of black and white
It dives
Underwater
A red eye
Searching
Searching
The flick of a tail
Or a fin
Gives away
An aquatic hiding-hole
The fish might try to dart away,
But snap!
It is caught
Trapped in a sharp beak.

–"Hunting Loon" by Sarah Goodwin, age 10

Common Loon

Gavia immer

A loon sighting at the cabin was rare throughout my childhood. We assumed the lake was too small for loons because they require a substantial aquatic runway to lift their heavy, densely-boned bodies from the water. Or, maybe the lake was big enough but the coffee-colored water obscured their vision and made hunting too difficult. Perhaps there were not adequate nesting sites to keep eggs safe from predators such as mink and raccoons. Whatever the reason, it was always a disappointment each spring when the cabin was opened, the ice out, the ducks and geese returned, but no loons. Occasionally, if we were lucky, a loon call would echo through the cool air at dusk as a stray loon visited the lake or simply flew overhead.

Is it possible not to be awed by the unusual and varied sounds of the loon? I always stop and listen when I hear them calling to one another. There are four types of loon calls: the soft, short hoot used to communicate with other loons about location; the wavering tremolo, sounding to some like a crazy laugh, used to communicate alarm or simply to announce the loon's presence; the yodel, a male territorial call which starts with three notes and ends with a swinging phrase unique to each caller; and the long, haunting wail, used to locate a partner and move closer together, like children playing Marco Polo in a pool. Though behavioral biologists have concluded the purpose of these four types of calls, I often think that it is with a mixture of hubris and ignorance that we draw such conclusions. We dismiss the lower animals' ability to communicate because of our own idea of communication and therefore we only try to describe their communication in terms that we understand. I suspect there may be complexities and subtleties to the loon's communication we miss entirely. For me it is enough that, from the distinct laugh to an imitation of a wolf pack, nothing says "Northwoods" better than two loons calling to one another from opposite sides of a lake as the day comes to a close, sun setting and first stars appearing in the twilight.

The first loon I saw at the cabin was more like a ghost. I was in the middle of the lake, alone in a canoe, surrounded by dense fog as the midsummer sun rose over the tall pines at the eastern edge of the lake. I heard the loon fly by. They are not silent flyers; their solid bones make them heavy enough to require high flapping rates to stay aloft. Then I heard the distinct loon call, and I think I saw its ghostly silhouette against the rising sun. Then it was gone.

The loon was ghost-like to the Ojibwe as well. They called the loon *Mang*, or "the most handsome of birds." Some believed the loon's haunting cry was an omen of death. In some legends, the loon has magical powers or serves as a messenger of power.

They are certainly powerful birds. The dense bones that make them such troubled flyers also make them superb divers—an essential trait for gathering food. They float by trapping air in their feathers, then let out the air and sink slowly until, with a push of their hind legs and an arch of their backs, they dive headfirst under the water. Once under the water, they are graceful swimmers, propelling themselves with their feet, wings tucked to their sides, quickly changing direction and catching prey, and using their sight to spy the flashes of sunlight reflecting off fish scales.

The evolution of these attributes that allow grace and ease in water has minimized the loon's terrestrial adaptation. Because their legs are far back on their bodies, it takes a great deal of effort to simply raise their breasts up off the ground. Walking up on shore is laborious enough, let alone building an intricate nest, thus they make nests which are really just mounds of sticks and mud near the shore.

In the last few years, a pair of loons has been nesting on the lake, and it is common to see them most of the summer out on the water, fishing, diving, and carrying their chicks on their back. My perspective on the presence of the loons only highlights the limitations of our concept of time within an ecosystem. It could be that loons come and go, with cycles of habitation that might last decades or even centuries. Why they have chosen these recent years to take up habitation on this lake I do not know.

Whether or not the loons remain inhabitants of this lake, I am glad for the opportunity to share this space with them, even if only for a short time. The loon teaches me that natural selection is all about compromise. In this case, grace and ease in the water come at the expense of terrestrial comfort. I suppose such evolutionary compromises are always the case. Relationships between family and friends, economic systems, and the workings of a clumsy democratic government are littered with impressive adaptations but also maladaptive compromises and unintended consequences. This is the nature of all systems and relationships it would seem. Though the result might be a water bird ill-equipped for land, family members having to learn the importance of giving one another grace, or elected officials having to accept other opinions, to do otherwise results in evolutionary dead ends, split families, and non-functioning government, the lesson would seem to be that holding intently onto an ideological position, just like holding onto a physical adaptation beyond the point of practicality, can only result in one thing: extinction.

And while I stood there I saw more than I can tell and I understood more than I saw; for I was seeing in a sacred manner the shapes of all things in the spirit, and the shape of all shapes as they must live together like one being.

—Black Elk, Oglala Lakota medicine man

Eastern Phoebe

Sayornis phoebe

The air is cool this morning. The screened porch faces the lake on the northern side of the cabin and is ten feet above the ground, and the lake surface is at least thirty feet lower down the hillside, giving me a false sense of elevation. I put on a second layer and set my book down periodically to warm my hands around my coffee mug. The sun has just risen, but the phoebe is already up and active. "Fee-bee" he calls, announcing his presence. His voice is raspy as if he still has sleep in his throat. His call is similar in duration and rhythm to the chickadee's two-note "spring-time," but without the clear tone. Sitting above the brush layer of the forest but below the canopy, I'm at eye level with the phoebe's preferred habitat. This level above the ground cover and the mammals inhabiting those niches and below the thick canopy of the trees, belongs to the flying creatures.

He moves from branch to branch around the deck. My presence this morning has roused him from the nest built earlier this spring on a support beam on the underside of the deck. He attracted his mate to the nest site with flying displays in which he spread his tail to show his genetic fitness. She must have been sufficiently impressed to choose him and his nesting site and, incidentally, to build the nest without any help from him. Their chicks have yet to fledge, so both parents are busy feeding them.

I presume that feeding the family is his purpose this morning. He is "hawking," sitting perched at the end of a branch, waiting to nab passing insects. When an insect comes within range, he quickly uses his aerobatics to catch his prey. These are the skills that his mate was selecting for when she looked at his tail, the key tool for these aerobatic maneuvers. She was not making a conscious choice. The females have evolved to prefer the male with the best tail for flying simply because the more females who chose good hunting males, the more offspring they produce that survives because of adequate food supply provided by the male. And since the chosen male had a good tail for flying, so did many of his offspring. This is an example of a positive feedback loop that is a basic principle in natural or sexual selection. In this case, sexual selection and natural selection pressured the evolution of the trait in the same direction. Sometimes the pressure works in opposite directions, which is often the case in songbirds, such as the bright red male cardinal, who sacrifices camouflage to attract the female.

Every now and then the phoebe reminds me of his name. "Fee-bee" he calls, flicking his tail to further express his annoyance with my company. Quite frankly, I do not understand his complaints. Our presence here has not deterred him from a nesting site. In fact, the opposite is true. The phoebes, like barn and cliff swallows, have not suffered from human intrusion into their habitats. Phoebes traditionally nested in the recesses of cliffs and rock ledges along streams. Looking around the cabin, I am not sure what natural site would have attracted a phoebe to these woods before cabins and other structures were built. There are hills, but the terrain does not offer cliffs, cuts in hillsides, or other natural nesting sites. Maybe they followed settlers into new habitats.

Phoebes are now equally at ease building a home in man-made recesses and ledges. It is good to be adaptable, especially as we continue to intrude into each other's space—though I would never consider him an intrusion into my morning reading time. "Fee-bee" he calls again. I am tempted to answer, "Timmm-eeee."

If I had influence with the good fairy who is supposed to preside over the christening of all children, I should ask that her gift to each child in the world be a sense of wonder so indestructible that it would last throughout life.

—Rachel Carson

Club Moss

Lycopodium obscurum

*L*ycopodium plants grow in the flat, open space below the great white pines down by the lake. This is where we camped in our leaky canvas tent before the cabin was built. The space is protected by trees, and the fallen needles and fescue grasses provided a good camping, picnic, and play space.

Club mosses have been growing in this space for as long as I have taken notice of the ground cover below the pines. They look like miniature pine trees but are more primitive and closely related to other seedless plants that populated the earth during the end of the Silurian period hundreds of millions of years ago, long before the seeded plants—angiosperms (those with flowers) and gymnosperms (those with cones)—became dominant. The Lycopods may have thrived for 200 million years earlier than the first ancestors of the great white pines that now protect them evolved.

Club mosses are perennials with deep roots, but grow only a few inches tall in the same spot each summer. My daughters, in their younger years, built little fairy houses and structures in the open areas of the pines. Sometimes they were simple lean-tos using the base of a pine for support. Other times, they were free-standing, multi-room dwellings made from scavenged twigs, grasses, bark and mosses. The most elaborate had pitched roofs, doors and windows. In their imaginings, the club mosses were grand trees on the front lawns of these dwellings for the butter-fly-like "fairies" that inhabit the woods around the cabin.

Ancestral plants to these club mosses were towering Lycopsid rainforests that reached their climax 325 million years ago. These ancestors have long been extinct, but what remains are genes passed through the generations to these modern-day plants, and the great coal beds made of fossilized remains of those ancestral forests in the Eastern United States and Europe that fuel so much of our modern electricity production.

These plants, then, represent the intricate exchange of matter in the history of our planet, connecting the living things such as plants and animals alive today with those of the past and with the nonliving components of the ecosystem. As the girls played around the club moss, they breathed out carbon dioxide, which might have been absorbed by these same plants. In turn, the plants provided the girls with oxygen and fodder for their imaginations and intellectual growth. It could be that the carbon my girls got from the sugars in their morning cereal and then exhaled after burning those sugars in their cells was once locked up in the coal from those fossilized plants in Pennsylvania. That carbon-containing coal may have been burned in coal-fired power plants that provided electricity to our homes, and then was released as carbon dioxide into the atmosphere, where it might have been absorbed by the wheat plants that ended up in our cereal.

I worry that too many children do not get the opportunity to create their own imaginary worlds while surrounded by the sights, sounds and smells of a forest, because we adults have taken over so much of their lives with playdates, organized sports and clubs, and the simple fear of letting them out of our sight in this world we often see as a place of danger. When I come across these primitive plants, I will always think of little girls building imaginary worlds for mythical creatures. And I will try never to be too educated or too cynical to see their fascinating symbiosis with the "primitive" covering of the forest floor, because I cannot think of a kind of play more important to the cognitive development of a young child. I am grateful they have had these experiences and that our family was fortunate enough to have the gift of this cabin and these woods. Unstructured time to play in the woods is more valuable than sports activities organized by parents and coaches, more important than family time at Disney World, and even more important than a guided nature hike led by someone like me.

The more clearly we can focus our attention on the wonders and realities of the universe about us, the less taste we shall have for destruction.

—Rachel Carson

Ruby-Throated Hummingbird

Archilochus colubris

The ruby-throated hummingbird is the only hummingbird found in the woods around the cabin and in the entire Great Lakes region. At first glance, hummingbirds appear to be the avian version of butterflies, or maybe even the inspiration for the fairies for which my daughters built little houses under the pines. But just as with people, initial judgments and stereotypes are often inaccurate.

These hummers are most often seen around the cabin deck, lured in by the feeder designed specifically for them. The males are easy to tell from the females as they have the characteristic iridescent red patch on their throats. Depending on the angle, this patch will appear red to black. The feathers are not red from pigment, but instead reflect the red portion of the spectrum due to texture.

It would be incorrect to think of these little fairy-like birds as simply docile consumers of flower nectar. As much as they eat the nectar from the flower (or the sugar water in the feeder), their tongue is W-shaped and brushy so that it can capture insects as well. Capturing a lot of nectar for the sugars and insects for the protein is necessary for survival. A hummingbird will eat its entire weight in food each day just to maintain its high rate of metabolism.

A hummer requires a high metabolism because it will beat its wings between sixty and two hundred times per second, and its heart will beat more than twelve hundred times per second. It has adapted its wings for tremendous aerobatic maneuvers, making it capable of flying in any direction and hovering with ease. This skill is necessary, because although you will often see hummingbirds perched on a branch near the feeder, you will not see them walking. Their feet are too small and light to support actual terrestrial movement. Therefore all of the movement of a hummingbird happens through the air.

To picture why hummingbirds can fly with the precision and grace that they do, it helps to remember that air is a fluid, like water, only thinner. It is not empty space. When I picture air in this manner, I can much more easily understand and visualize the movement of the hummingbird and compare it to a graceful aquatic animal like a dolphin. When they hover, they are really "treading air" like a swimmer treads water. The wing can rotate 180 degrees, just like a swimmer's hand rotates back and forth as he paddles in the water to remain stationary. The wing of a hummingbird is designed for creating lift equally whether moving backward or forward, allowing a hummingbird to fly in any direction and hover more efficiently than the most efficient helicopter.

Hovering, darting and zipping past the red feeder with a tiny helicopter-like buzz is where these birds are mostly found at the cabin. However, it is unlikely to see two feeding at the same time. Do not be fooled by the dainty structure of these birds. They are quite aggressive and territorial. They do not share food and will readily dive-bomb and chase off other hummingbirds from the feeder, resulting in an impressive aerial dogfight display between two individuals.

It is the female that has the most immediate need for the food since she is the one raising the chicks in the nest that is probably near the feeder. The female chooses the nest site, builds the nest, and feeds the chicks two to three times an hour for up to twenty-two days before the babies fledge. These mothers are as industrious as any in the bird world. At night they settle in for sleep, at which time they will often go into a state of torpor, or hibernation, for a few hours. Otherwise they would starve to death before the next dawn.

It is not just for their daily activities that they require considerable caloric intake; it is important to remember that these are migratory birds. They spend most of the winter in southern Mexico and Central America. Some hummingbirds actually migrate across the Gulf of Mexico, traversing the five hundred miles in about twenty hours. Accomplishing this feat requires doubling their body fat, which equates to an extra gram of fat. This is the fuel for this marathon flight. It is difficult to imagine any bird keeping up one hundred to two hundred wingbeats and twelve hundred heartbeats per second, completing such a journey. When this animal is moving, it is beating its wings at full speed continuously for the entire pilgrimage; it does not have the ability to glide like the monarch butterfly can do when it makes a similar journey. Clearly this little bird comes with many surprises and amazing adaptations. But then, so do all individuals of all species. Each is unique and equally as adapted to survival, and therefore, I think, deserving of the opportunity to not only survive, but also thrive.

Overhead—the sound of wings on air
Or in the nest tending chicks with care
Maybe a long screech across the bay
Or high above on a sunny day
Aweing, humbling and majestic—our eagles

Bald Eagle

Haliaeetus leucocephalus

We always check on the status of the eagles after arriving at the cabin. Are they still there? How is the nest? For years, a pair of bald eagles has nested across the bay in front of the cabin, atop a tall pine tree. The nest grew larger and larger each year, expanding up and out, perched on the broken trunk of a tall pine like a giant, twiggy, buttercup. A few years ago, half of the nest fell away, probably because of a storm combined with its own weight. The eagles still nested there that spring. More recently, they have begun to build a nest thirty feet from the cabin, twenty feet from the shoreline and only a few feet above our visual line when standing on the screened porch. What made them decide to build a new home? And did they decide this together, or did one start building the new nest and the other simply followed?

The eagles appear to be partial to the tall pines ringing the lake's edge. From this perch, the eagle has the vantage point needed as a predator, peering into the water for fish, the prey it feeds on almost exclusively. Plus, it only seems proper for a bird of this majesty to occupy great perches above all the other creatures below. Its brown body and white head with yellow beak contrast with the dark green of the pines and the bright blue of a sunny sky. I always pause to watch when they stop to rest in the pines towering over the club moss between the cabin and the lakefront. It is impossible to think of their presence as routine.

They are a species that follows strict routines. They return to the same nest each year and keep the same mate for life. They fish in the same waters. And once every year, one flies upside down under its mate. They lock talons and hang on, somehow defying gravity while conducting a mid-air dance. The female usually lays two eggs each spring, producing two chicks. It takes a year or two for the juvenile to get its distinctive white head. Often only one chick survives; the stronger of the two out-competes the other for food from the parents. If one dies, it is not usually from starvation or attack by the dominant chick, but instead it simply lacks the strength to survive when the parents push it from the nest for its inaugural flight. It sounds cruel, but this is exactly the kind of behavior that Charles Darwin predicted. More offspring than can survive are produced so that they compete for resources, and the fittest survive to pass on those traits. Being able to out-compete one's siblings for food from the day of hatching is certainly an advantageous trait.

One to two offspring a year per mating pair easily sustains the population, as opposed to the dozen or so that small birds such as a nuthatch or chickadee produce each year. A long-lived, large predator at the top of the food chain requires a great deal of calories to sustain it. There simply is not enough energy flowing up the food chain to support more than a few large predators in an ecosystem. All of the energy in the ecosystem is captured and converted from light energy into chemical energy by the plants. Most of this energy is lost to the atmosphere as the light energy is converted to chemical energy and stored as matter in the plant's body. Only about ten percent of the energy passes to the predator. At each step up the food chain this happens—ninety percent of the energy is used and eventually lost as heat and ten percent is stored and passed upward. The further up the food chain, the larger the organism and the fewer that can be supported by the level below. Ecologists often represent this in the form of a pyramid, with the producers on the bottom and the top predator, such as an eagle, alone on the top.

Top predators are thought of as the "strongest" or the "rulers" of the ecosystems they inhabit. But while living at the top of the food chain ensures safety from other predators, it comes at a cost. These top predators are actually the most susceptible to the impact of toxins introduced into the ecosystem. At the bottom of the food chain, a toxin is spread among the entire population, which could be millions of individuals. Toxins are passed up the food chain as predator eats prey, and they accumulate at higher levels in each predator's body.

This is what happened with DDT in the 1950s and 1960s. It devastated the populations of birds of prey like bald eagles. The toxin accumulated in the birds' bodies and made egg shells too thin and fragile to withstand the environment. The bald eagle was nearly lost until pioneers like Rachel Carson led a fight against the industries and government offices that had declared in advertising campaigns that "DDT was good for you and me." Our national symbol was nearly lost to ignorance about a pesticide and the interactions of the food web.

The bald eagle is more than just a symbol of the United States. Like a lion is to the grassy African plains, the bald eagle is the iconic figure of the Northwoods. Because of this, it has had spiritual importance for every group of people that has lived on this continent. Many American Indian tribes hold the eagle as sacred. Most Native American cultures consider the eagles to be birds with impressive power or "medicine," with a role in guiding tribal leaders, and even as a messenger between humans and the Creator. Great significance is placed on the collecting and keeping of an eagle feather. The feathers are used in the construction of dream catchers, where they represent a symbol of breath or air. A baby watching the air playing with the feather on the dream catcher above her cradleboard is entertained and also receives a lesson on the importance of good air.

I understand the awe from an encounter with this bird and the reverence for such a powerful predator. As a boy, I was canoeing alone when I had my first close encounter with the cabin eagles. I looked skyward as an eagle passed overhead. It was only ten to twenty feet in the air. I do not know what made me look up, as I had not heard a sound. Its wings spanned at least six feet. It seemed as if it could have plucked me out of the canoe without much effort with its massive beak and muscular talons. It humbled me. I was stunned and amazed, and simply sat and drifted on the calm water as I absorbed the experience. And to think that actions our species took years ago to rid ourselves of insect pests nearly eradicated this symbol so sacred to so many groups of people—be they pledging allegiance to a flag topped with an eagle, sleeping under the protection of a dream catcher, or floating quietly on a Northern Wisconsin lake, awed into silent reverence.

The original master carpenter
Raw materials of sticks and mud
Woven dams and all-season lodges
She swims silently to and fro accumulating
A cache of tree tops for winter's approach
Ignoring my observing eyes
Until I come just a little too close
Then...THWACK!
Her mighty tail crashes down on the water's surface
And she is gone and all around are warned

Beaver

Castor canadensis

Beavers are master carpenters. During the summer, when the air is warm and the water is still, I canoe around their lodges, investigating the intricate construction that will stand beyond the time it is inhabited. They first construct a superstructure of vertical poles. Next, sticks, grass and mud are woven horizontally, thickening the walls that protect them and their pups from predators and the elements year-round. Their lodges remind me of the heavy rafters that rest on the even larger center beam that supports the cabin roof.

Beavers do not hibernate, so they create a cache of treetops in front of the lodge, just below the surface of the water. The larger branches and trunks are for their construction projects, but they prefer to eat the tops of the trees that are tender and rich in nutrients from new growth. The purpose of the dam is to make the water deep enough so that when the lake freezes over they can swim out under the ice and access their cache of food. I cannot fathom the evolutionary steps and genetic inheritance that led the beaver to discover that it could use a dam to create deep enough water to provide a safe place to inhabit and keep food accessible year-round.

Beavers are surprisingly big, though usually one sees just a beaver's head above the waterline as it swims silently along, with the telltale V-shaped wake spreading behind it. Because of this limited view, most people think of them as fairly small rodents. However, their dense bodies weigh up to seventy pounds and are about three feet long including the tail. They swim stealthily until they suspect danger is near, and then they reveal their size and power with a thunderous whack of their tail against the water's surface.

In the winter, I have crept in my snowshoes to an active beaver lodge. An active lodge is recognizable by the chimney of ice crystals made by the escaping heat and moisture from their metabolic processes. If you sneak up quietly and thump your snowshoe on the side of the lodge and listen, you can hear the splash as they leave the lodge and escape into the water below the ice. For the beaver, retreating to safety means willingly diving into the icy water, away from the lumbering sounds of the bundled-up, snowshoe-fitted threat whose greatest fear at that moment is falling through the ice. The beaver is protected from the barely above-freezing water by its fur and layer of fat, while the snowshoer would succumb to hypothermia in minutes. One species' paradise is another's hell.

Though our two species may be separated by a layer of ice, beavers and humans share a long history of interaction. It is because of the Europeans' penchant for various products derived from the beaver pelt that the French-Canadian voyageurs explored and expanded into the Great Lakes region of North America and came into contact with the Ojibwe. There were three main materials from the beaver skins used in clothing production: the full pelt (fur and skin), leather or suede (the skin with all fur removed), and felts (removing the fur from the pelt, and processing it with heat and pressure to form a piece of pliable material). Beaver pelts were used extensively in hat making because of their strength and malleability. It may not be a stretch to say that if not for the Europeans' love of a good hat, the relationship between the French voyageurs and the Ojibwe would not have formed, or at least would not have formed when it did. But the love for hats was there, so they formed a long-standing relationship that resulted in wartime alliances, many marriages, and the exchange of goods and cultural traditions. It also meant the introduction of many European-borne illnesses, such as smallpox, against which the Ojibwe and other indigenous peoples of North America had no immunity.

Beaver are still readily trapped in the Great Lakes region. By the early 1900s the value of this commodity was high enough that the beaver was trapped nearly to extinction, however, during the last one hundred years the beaver has made a remarkable comeback. The pelt is not as valuable as it once was. However, many still actively run trap lines throughout much of the winter. It is not easy work, as it requires knowing the beaver habitat well enough to know where to chop through the ice and place traps, which means the trapper is in danger of slipping into the ice-water habitat of the beaver.

Years ago, I spent January of my sophomore year in college at the University of Minnesota field station at Lake Itasca State Park in Northwest Minnesota studying winter ecology. Another student and I wanted to study the carrion eating habits of Northwoods animals. But what to use for bait? We found our answer with a local trapper. He had a pile of frozen, skinned, beaver carcasses in his front lawn stacked like firewood, and we were welcome to as many as we could fit in our car. The look on our classmates' faces was one of amusement with a little disgust when we returned to our cabin with a dozen or so "naked" beaver carcasses stuffed into the back of a 2-door Ford Escort. Needless to say, we drove back to the park without the heat running. We placed the carcasses throughout the park, establishing a "carrion line." Each morning we would ski the route, observing while hidden among the trees and then inspecting the carrion site for signs of animals in the snow. Turns out, the species that relied mostly on the carrion in the dead of winter was chickadees and woodpeckers. Of course we had to consider that most Northwoods mammals and birds did not evolve to feed on skinned beaver in the middle of the forest. There was only one instance of a mammal feeding on any of the carcasses. Coincidentally, there was a mink living in a tree thirty feet behind our cabin where we placed one carcass. All that time skiing miles of carrion line and the most exciting find could be viewed from our cabin window.

The beaver is more than just an important product of trade. The natural life cycle of the beaver results in the transformation of waterways utilized for transportation. A beaver dam can convert a small stream into a pond, lake or deeper waterway navigable by canoe. The Ojibwe also valued the beaver's meat as well as the fur. The tail, which was rich in fat and calories, was especially prized during the long, harsh winters.

The Ojibwe people are also connected to the beaver before (and beyond) its value as a commodity. The Ojibwe myth of how the beaver got its flattened, fat-filled tail is a story warning against bravado and self-righteousness. According to the story, the beaver originally had a big, fluffy tail which brought him immense pride. He became angered by the other animals' lack of envy over his tail. In anger, the beaver began cutting down trees until he cut one too big to manage and it fell on his tail, smashing it flat. The Creator told him that a beaver is not liked for his tail but for his kindness and wisdom, and also told him how to use his flat tail. "Now your tail will help you swim rapidly," the Creator said, "and when you want to signal a message to a friend, all you have to do is slap your tail on the water."

The message for those of us who dwell above the ice as the beaver swims below is obvious. Vanity is energy wasted.

Headfirst down the tree

The little white-breasted picks her way

Most ascend

She descends

Requiring even special toes

What others miss while reaching higher

The nuthatch finds picking her way lower

White-Breasted Nuthatch

Sitta carolinensis

Nuthatches live their entire lives in one territory and always in pairs, though like most songbirds, they are probably only socially monogamous, and then only for one breeding season. They are most noticeable when the leaves have fallen from the trees and most of the other birds have left the Northwoods for warmer climates. They can be found chasing off other nuthatches while mixed in with flocks of chickadees, preferring the company of the black and white sentinel of the woods.

Nuthatches are unassuming little birds. They quietly go about their business, scaling up and down and around the trunks of one tree and the next. They do not have a call that fills the woods with song, nor one that serves a great warning to others. Just a simple, rapid "Wa wa wa wa wa." It is a call more like one would imagine coming from an undersized, overly-excited crow unable to say his hard "C's" as a means to attract a mate.

These birds spend most of their time on the sides of trees, foraging in the cracks of the bark for insects. But unlike most every other insect-eating bird, they almost always work their way down the trunk headfirst. Their feet are "backward" for this purpose, with the back toe and claw much longer than the front toes and claws. They spend most of their time, then, with their head tilted out ninety degrees from the direction of their spine. They move effortlessly up and down, back and forth, and around the trunk of the tree as easily as a robin hops around a well-manicured lawn. It could be that this method of foraging for food allows the nuthatch to spot food other species of birds miss.

There is a principle in ecology called the mutual exclusion principle, which basically states that two species cannot indefinitely inhabit the same niche within a habitat. This principle is a driving force in the great diversity of life that has evolved on this planet. If there is an empty niche in an ecosystem, it will be filled eventually with a well-adapted species. As the individuals within a population of a species compete for resources, one variant will always thrive and the others will move on, evolve, or die out. Having the ability to see things differently is one way to thrive. Nature rewards uniqueness, whether that be a unique physical trait or a unique way of looking at the world—or, in the nuthatch's case, both.

What's in a name? That which we call a rose by any other name would smell as sweet.

—Juliet from Shakespeare's Romeo and Juliet

Chipping Sparrow

Spizella passerine

To many people, any small brown bird is simply a sparrow. To broadly apply such a name is to deny each species its individuality. Each species is the result of thousands or, more likely, millions of years of natural selection. The branching family trees of these species are the result of subtle adaptations to subtle environmental changes, fueled by even more subtle genetic changes that result from random mutations and the mixing of populations. I would not want to deny the chipping sparrow its heritage.

The chipping sparrow is the result of this process just like all other life on Earth. At only five inches at best, it is the smallest of its sparrow cousins in North America. It is an energetic little bird, bouncing around the woodpile, gathering insects and seeds for its meal. Maybe he is making a contribution to nest-building by distracting attention away from the female as she does the hard work—although she is not a terribly impressive architect. Their little nests are so flimsy I can see through them. They are little more than small cups of dried grasses lined with animal hair and fine plant material. But they are adequate enough to house three to five eggs that will incubate for eleven to fourteen days. Once hatched, the chicks will live in the nest, fed by both parents for ten to twelve days before moving out.

Seeing the chipping sparrow, I pause and notice its individuality, appreciating the result of millions of years of natural selection that makes it specific to the niche that it fills. As long as the chippy occupies this niche, no other species will. This is another example of the competitive exclusion principle, which states that two species cannot occupy the same niche in an ecosystem. One will always evolve or go extinct. It is good to have a role and to know what it is, be it in an ecosystem, classroom, workplace, or family. My ultimate goal as both an educator and a parent is for my children and my students to know who they are and who they wish to be, and ultimately how they wish to live in the world. Knowing one's strengths and weaknesses, and then how to work with and overcome them is crucial to this outcome. In the end, when all the individuals in a community know their role, then they can know what their contribution can be to that community. And then, with collaboration, so much more can be achieved as a collective than as individuals.

The world, we are told, was made especially for humans—a presumption not supported by all the facts...Why should humanity value itself more than a small part of the one great unit of creation?

—John Muir

White Pine

Pinus strobus

Majestic white pines ring the edge of the lake. Some of the tallest provide a protective canopy over the fire pit and picnic area near the waterfront. The shoreline of this lake is defined by these giants that survived the last mass logging in Sawyer County. When I was younger, I would climb up one as far as I dared to go. I never made it more than halfway, but was left with pine tar on my hands as a trophy of my great conquest just the same.

These trees can reach over one hundred feet tall and three to four feet in diameter. Because they keep their needle-like leaves throughout the entire winter season, they provide continual shelter for small mammals and birds. One on the north side of the bay directly across from the cabin served as the perch for an eagle's nest that was active for at least thirty years, only just recently succumbing to bad weather. During that time, the grand tree has remained essentially unchanged, as these thirty years of observation is only a fraction of its possible 200-year lifespan. These trees are identifiable not only by their height and somewhat triangular shape, but also their soft appearance. The needles come in bundles of five, are three to five inches long, and are softer to the touch and a lighter shade of green than the needles of a red pine, making them appear softer and less rugged than the other large pine species in the Northwoods.

White pines are gymnosperms, meaning "naked seeds," because their seeds are not grown inside the safety of a flower or fruit (like an apple). Gymnosperms evolved before flowering plants, but after mossy plants such as the Lycopods of which the club moss is an example. Instead of producing a flower for pollination or relying on fruit to carry a seed to the ground, the gymnosperms protect the seeds in cones. Some have cones that require the heat of a forest fire to open them; others open up and drop the seeds directly after pollination. In white pines, the female cones are four to six inches long, with thin and far-spread scales, each containing two small, winged seeds that use wind to propel themselves away from the parent.

The Ojibwe made a glue-like pitch from the gummy sap that flows from under the bark when it is removed. Cooked down until thick and then mixed with charcoal, this pitch was used to seal the seams of birch bark canoes. The bark itself was cooked and pounded into a mash for treating gangrenous wounds and other infections. When that sap stained my hands after a daring climb, it stayed until I either scrubbed it off with a stiff brush or removed it with a petroleum-based solvent such as gasoline or turpentine. If neither of these was readily available, then the next best solution was to rub my hands in dirt. The fine dust in the soil would stick to the pine tar, leaving dirty patches on my hand, but solving the stickiness problem, which was all I really needed to avoid interrupting my outdoor playtime around these grandfathers of the woods.

White settlers, however, found the most use for these trees during the mid-to-late 1800s. All conifers grow with a single, central terminal trunk, providing for straight-grained wood and long boards. The soft wood of the white pine makes it easy to mill into everything from matches to boards for building homes. It is still grown and logged for those purposes. The family cabin is sided with locally-grown pine, logged and milled into siding that is one quarter of a log, giving the appearance of whole logs from the outside.

One hundred and fifty years ago, great logging camps were assembled each winter. The lumberjacks worked through the winter felling the trees, loaded them onto sleds and pulled them to the rivers. When spring came, the "river rats" floated the logs down to the mill. This method of transportation limited logging to the winter season and to where adequate river transportation was available. With the introduction of the railroad in the latter half of the nineteenth century, the remainder of this region was opened up to the logging companies. This expansion of the logging industry led to the loss of virgin forests. Most of the current forests in Sawyer County—and, indeed, almost all of Wisconsin and Minnesota—have been clear-cut at some point in the past and regrown. The few white pines ringing the lake escaped the clear-cutting, probably because they were not part of a stand of similar trees and it was not worth the expense of logging so few trees.

I do not know the age of my old climbing tree or how many board feet of lumber exist inside its trunk. A swing now hangs on a cross board that bridges the gap between one of the white pines and a neighboring tree. The swing is positioned just where the hill falls away a few feet to the lakeshore so swingers—children and adults alike—feel much higher than they actually are. I hope it stays there for years to come so that my children can push their children out toward the water and watch them swing back again. Maybe one of them will, inspired by the white pine itself, climb all the way to the top.

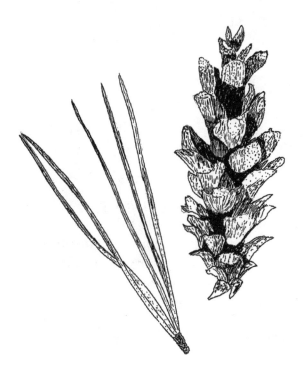

O Christmas Tree, O Christmas Tree,
Your branches green delight us!
They are green when summer days are bright,
They are green when winter snow is white.
O Christmas Tree, O Christmas Tree,
Your branches green delight us!

—English version of German Christmas song by Ernst Anschütz

Balsam Fir

Abies balsamea

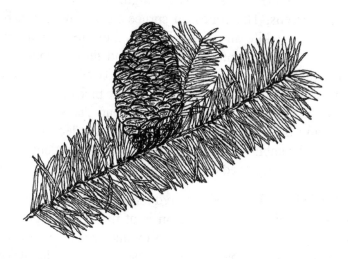

Not all coniferous trees are pine trees. In fact, many of the trees most people would call "pine" trees are actually more likely to be spruce or fir trees. The easiest way to tell the trees apart is by a closer examination of their leaves. Conifers do have leaves, though they are called needles, and they do lose their leaves, but not every year like deciduous trees. Instead they continuously lose and replace their needles a few at a time rather than all at once, which is why coniferous trees are also called "evergreens." Pine trees have rounded needles that are in clumps of two to five. Spruce and fir needles are not in clumps; each needle originates from its own bud on the branch. Additionally, spruce trees have needles that feel square when rolled between your fingers, while fir needles feel flat and cannot be rolled between your fingers. An easy way to remember this rule is that *s*pruce equals *s*quare, and *f*ir equals *f*lat.

Coniferous trees can also be differentiated by their reproductive structures. All the coniferous trees have cones, but the position of the cones helps distinguish the different groups of evergreens. The cones on spruce trees hang down below the branch, while on balsam fir trees they stand up above the branch and also contain both male and female cones on the same tree. Balsam fir trees are usually twenty to thirty years old before they begin to produce cones, which open and release their "naked" seeds within the same year. The seeds are eaten by many bird species, including the chickadees so common around the cabin, as well as red squirrels, as evidenced by the piles of dropped seeds left behind at the base of these trees.

The balsam firs grow scattered throughout the woods around the cabin, although this region is at the lower edge of their growing range. They are fast-growing, and even considered to be a weed tree by many. Because they can tolerate shade, they are often found growing under the cover of larger white and red pines. Balsam firs require moist soil. Because the soil around the cabin is mostly sand and glacial till, in this ecosystem they are limited to growing near the water, and then only grow to be about six inches in diameter. Trees further north can get to eighteen inches in diameter and up to fifty feet tall, with the single, straight main stem characteristic to all of the gymnosperms.

There are many uses for components of the tree, but wood from this species is mostly used for pulp wood, as it is generally too small to be used for lumber. The tree itself is a popular choice as a Christmas tree because, in addition to its ideal shape, the needles are relatively soft and fragrant, and will stay on the tree after it is cut.

There are more historical and practical uses for parts of this tree. According to some sources, every part of the balsam was used by Native Americans. They used the yellowish oleoresin to treat influenza, scurvy, burns, wounds, sores, and bruises and to repair canoe holes. Tea from the needles was good for treating colds, coughs, and asthma. The French voyageurs learned to collect the resin from Native Americans and then sold it back east and in Europe to generate seasonal income. The thin, blistered, grayish bark of the balsam releases rich, fragrant sap, hence the common name of "blister pine." The resin that is released was used for many years as the medium to hold and preserve specimens on microscope slides sold to research labs and schools. The resin was also sold as chewing gum before more modern chewing gum from the chicle tree was introduced to the marketplace by William Wrigley, Jr. The resin can also be used for first aid and, there are stories of loggers sealing up cuts and injuries with resin from the balsam fir and then going right back to work. My brother and I would like to say that Dad worked us so hard when building the cabin that he used this technique to keep us working as we got cuts and bruises, but we would be exaggerating—though we still use family gatherings to complain about how early he would wake us up because there was always a project to be completed. In retrospect, I am not sure that the accuracy of teenage boys' memories can be trusted in regards to such complaints.

Life at the cabin is never so precarious that we need to utilize the local balsam firs for such purposes. Here they simply add to the ecosystem by providing year-round cover for many species, from the small chickadee to the white-tailed deer, and also add to the aesthetic of the dense stands of "pine" trees that make up much of the shoreline of Barker Lake.

The solitary aspen groans and creaks
As the storm pushes and pulls
Ripping leaves and severing limbs
Until no longer can the roots hold
Tight to the rocks and sand
The solitary tree falls
And sunlight once again reaches
The forest floor

Quaking Aspen

Populus tremuloides

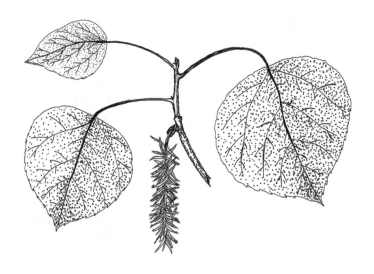

When I walk through these woods around the cabin, it is a dense canopy of mostly maple, basswood and even some oak. Thirty years ago, these same woods had a very different texture and feel to them. When we first started building the cabin, the canopy of this forest was mostly made up of aspen leaves flapping back and forth, flashing between two shades of green in the summer breeze.

The flattened shape of the aspen's petiole, or leaf stem, causes the leaves to do their characteristic "tremble" in the slightest breeze, hence the name quaking aspen. The stem is shaped like a tiny airfoil, creating a tiny area of low pressure on one side of the stem, just like the curvature of an airplane wing lowers the air pressure on the upper side of the wing as air takes the longer path over the top. As the wind rushes over the petiole, that energy twists the petiole, which is really shaped like a two-sided wing, therefore causing the stem to swing from one side and then the other in an alternating fashion. This energy is transferred down to the leaf, which waves back and forth like a float-rider waving to a crowd during a parade. Recently, a researcher found that the trembling action of the leaves may help deter insect damage as the constant movement prevents the insects from finding firm footing. In autumn, the leaves become brilliantly golden as the green chlorophyll gets used up in the shortening days before the tree finally lets the leaves go and they fall, coating the forest floor, bathing the forest in a subdued yellow hue in the late afternoon sun.

I can close my eyes and imagine a very different forest a few generations ago. Quaking aspen and the similar big-toothed aspen are trees that thrive in sunlight. Because of this they are often the first trees to take advantage of an opening left by a forest fire, major windstorm, or clear-cutting lumber practices. These trees grow quickly and have a relatively short life span. A few pioneer seeds carried in by wind can sprout and grow into a population that quickly becomes the keystone species in the region.

Unlike most deciduous trees, aspen trees are either male or female, but not both. They begin producing the catkins—which in females are pendulous, flower-producing structures—in about four years, and maximize seed production in about fifty years before completing their life cycle. Pollinators transfer sperm from the male tree to the nearby female flower, and an embryo containing seeds is produced. Each seed is lightweight enough to be easily carried by the wind and is viable enough to germinate in rather poor soil and open sunlight.

It is not their sexual reproduction practices, however, that allowed the aspens to become the dominant species at one time in these woods. Aspens rapidly spread by using asexual reproduction. After some type of disturbance, a single root system will send up new shoots called suckers. While they may look like separate trees, they are actually extensions of the same individual; therefore one forest, many acres in size, could in reality be genetically just one individual organism, each shoot a clone from the original seedling that took root in a sunny spot generations ago. A giant clone named Pando in south-central Utah covers more than 17 acres and is comprised of 47 thousand individual stems. This "cloning" strategy leads to a kind of immortality, for though the individual shoots might complete their life cycle in fifty years, the organism can continue to produce new shoots for thousands, maybe even a million years.

Many years ago, my brother and I built a small, triangular-shaped treehouse between three mature aspen trees. We got as far as building a solid floor for the treehouse, but never finished the project. What is it about kids and treehouses? I understand the desire for kids to have a separate place to call their own out from under the protective wing of Mom and Dad. But why do kids prefer the elevation of a treehouse over an easier-to-build fort on the ground? Had we attempted that strategy I suspect we would have had a greater chance of completing the project. Maybe the desire for elevation is the result of an expression of some ancestral genes we all carry, exerting themselves in an attempt to separate ourselves from the dangers of night-time ground-dwelling creatures.

Had my brother and I understood the biology of these trees, we would have recognized the short-sightedness of attaching a permanent structure to the trunks of elder shoots from the larger colony of aspen trees inhabiting this forest and nearing the end of their lifespan. These individual shoots grow quickly, elevating their treetops higher and higher to capture the sun's energy. This strategy, while effective at gathering energy and colonizing a clear space, is not without its downside. This tall stature, with the majority of its branches and leaves at the top— giving it a shape like an extremely tall dandelion—coupled with a relatively small root ball anchor, causes each individual shoot to be highly susceptible to wind storms.

This vulnerability became obvious on our property not too long ago. When we drove down the two hundred-yard driveway to the cabin one morning in late spring, we could immediately see that something was amiss. The eight-by-ten foot deck that should have been attached to the side of the screened porch was scattered on the ground in a mass of splintered deck boards, spindles, and joists. The small structure had been ripped from the side of the cabin as if a giant bear had taken a swipe at it, severing the whole thing. When the forest is made up of large stands of individual tall aspens, they all move and sway together in the wind. When a gap is opened in their collective, an individual, such as the one bordering the open space created by the construction of the cabin, loses the support of its sibling shoots. Fortunately, when the eighteen inch diameter quaking aspen had blown over and crushed the deck, it left the rest of the cabin untouched.

This is how a forest undergoes succession from one kind of forest to another. As open areas are created in the stand of aspen shoots, the super-organism spreading through the roots in the ground will either fill the space with new aspen shoots or, as in the case of the woods around the cabin, a second wave of tree species succeeds the aspens and begins to transform the forest into a maple–basswood forest. For the aspens it becomes a house of cards. A few fall, weakening the collective, and as more fall the remaining aspens are left alone as the forest shifts to a maple–basswood forest with a few solitary aspen trees reaching above the new canopy. These solitary trees are no match for summer thunderstorms.

In brief moments when I can see beyond the limitations of my own life span, I understand this forest not as just a collection of individual species, but as an organism itself. It grows and develops from one kind of forest to another, always maintaining the homeostasis of the greater ecosystem rooted in the sandy and rocky soil below my feet as I walk these woods, just like an individual organism begins as a single cell and undergoes miraculous changes throughout its life cycle.

In a way, aspen forests can be a victim of their own success. The seeds require plenty of sunlight to sprout and thrive. But the mature aspen stand that successfully colonizes the open spaces after a perturbation monopolizes the resources, leaving little chance for its own offspring to germinate and grow. For new aspen offspring to succeed, they must leave the forest of their origin to spread and colonize additional space. The aspen's life cycle requires an evolutionary strategy of pioneerism and pilgrimage.

As I walk through this forest, once mostly aspens, it is hard not to see parallels with our own history of colonization, westward expansion and manifest destiny. This parallel begins with the shift ten to fifteen thousand years ago from hunting and gathering and herding to agricultural settlements. The concentration of and increase in food production led to a population increase, which in turn required spreading onto more land, converting that land into agricultural use to support the increase in population, and still more colonization of existing ecosystems.

Fast forward ten thousand years or so, give or take a few millennia, and in the northern Great Lakes region the Ojibwe have settled in this area after moving from the northeast region of North America. They displaced many of the Lakota that lived here before them, only to then be largely displaced and confined to isolated reservations by European settlers spreading westward in the 1800s. It was this last group that did the most to remake this landscape. Much of the region that was predominantly white and red pine was clear-cut for lumber and then turned into farmland. As settlements developed in one region, more settlements spread out, clear-cutting more land for resources and farmland just like an aspen super-organism becomes the predominant species in a region, growing up so tall and thick as to prevent their own offspring from taking root in that same region.

Ironically, it was the actions of the European settlers clearing a region and then leaving it fallow that allowed the aspens in many of the local forests to take hold. It is still occurring today in the region around the cabin.

Land that was once farmed is left to return to forest, and within a few years the first aspens take root and begin to fill the open sky with their spreading canopy. The resulting stand of aspen will eventually become one of these nearly immortal stands of aspen, or succumb to windstorms, leaving openings for the maples and basswoods to slowly succeed them. This is a story without an ending, just transitions from one keystone species to the next, to the next, and to the next.

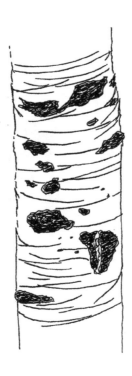

The nation behaves well if it treats its natural resources as assets which it must turn over to the next generation increased, and not impaired, in value.

—Theodore Roosevelt

Black Bear

Ursus americana

The black bear is the largest predator in the Great Lakes region. Though larger than the timber wolf, it does not share the wolf's status as a top predator in this ecosystem. Black bears are truly omnivorous. They will eat just about anything: roots, leaves, berries, insects, grass, small mammals, deer and even livestock. They have powerful jaws, damaging claws, and the strength to kill large prey, though that happens quite rarely. They do not have the same speed, endurance, and advantage of the pack that allow wolves to efficiently take down such large prey as deer or moose. It is simply easier and more energy efficient to eat things like insects, roots, and grasses that do not require an exertion of great amounts of energy.

Black bears are solitary animals with a large range, though they do interact socially during the spring mating season. But after mating occurs, the males and females go separate ways. Because mating season is almost a full year ahead of when it would be most advantageous for cubs to be born, the fertilized egg from the spring mating does not actually implant into the uterus until fall, effectively delaying birth until the next spring.

Once the days and nights begin to cool in the fall, the bear will seek out a suitable den in which to hibernate through the coldest part of the winter. They find small caves, burrows, or even the spaces opened up by the upturned root ball of a newly fallen aspen. The black bear spends its summer eating whatever it can find to build up a fat layer to fuel the upcoming extended sleep, though it can and will awaken during the winter, if necessary, to forage for food. Through this winter sleep, they deplete their fat reserves, and the expectant mother continues to gestate her soon-to-be-born cub. The cub will stay with the mother for more than a year and hibernate with her its first winter, so the female will only mate every other year. When it is time to emerge from the den, the bear's metabolism increases and it begins to burn the high energy brown fat stored in the upper region of its back. This fat is calorie-rich and produces more heat than the rest of the lighter fat in the bear's body. The burning of this high-energy, centrally-located fat raises the bear's core body temperature, bringing it out of hibernation.

We humans have a long history of admiring the bear. The Ojibwe call the black bear Mukwa and have many stories about the bear, including a story of the Sleeping Bear Sand Dunes in Northern Michigan. Before the two-leggeds inhabited this land, according to the story, the four-legged creatures could speak to one another. A black bear mother and two cubs caught in a forest fire retreated to the safety of the cold water of Lake Michigan. The mother swam further into the lake but her cubs fell behind and were overcome by the cold water. In her grief and dedication to her cubs she waited an entire year for them to find her. The Great Spirit was so moved by her devotion that he placed her on the shore to become a giant sand dune and raised two islands, Little and Big Manitou, where the cubs disappeared so that the mother could always keep watch over her lost cubs.

Another legend explains the origin of the bear's short tail. Bear once had a long tail, of which he could be very proud. One winter day, Bear met Otter fishing through a hole in the ice and was envious of the large pile of fish Otter had caught. Bear asked how to catch such fish, and the mischievous otter decided to trick Bear, and told Bear that the secret to catching fish was to dangle one's tail through a hole in the ice as bait, holding it there until a fish bites, and then to quickly flip the fish out of the hole onto the cold ice above the safety of the water. Otter then graciously allowed Bear to use his fishing hole and took his pile of fish and left Bear to his fishing. Bear was persistent and sat patiently with his tail in the icy water. He waited all day and into the cold night until the time he finally gave up, only to realize that his tail was stuck in the now frozen-over-hole in the ice. He pulled and pulled, eventually breaking off his tail. Bears have had short tails ever since. A fool and his tail shall soon be parted I guess, with the moral being not to believe all that you hear—even when coming from one as convincing as Otter.

Many Ojibwe have held the black bear as a kindred spirit because its paw prints are similar to human footprints. Unlike other mammals that walk on their toes, bears, like humans, leave prints that are plantograde, meaning the whole of the foot is placed on the ground with each step.

Additionally, when a bear stands on its hind legs, his front legs resemble human arms and hands. Another legend tells of an older man bow-hunting for deer and becoming lost while tracking the deer for several miles. While crossing a frozen lake he fell through the ice. Having pulled himself free of the icy water he had to quickly warm himself or succumb to hypothermia. He was saved by finding a hibernating bear and curling up next to the bear for warmth until he was dry and warm enough to venture back into the cold to find his way home. When he finally arrived home, he told his wife of his stay with Brother Bear.

In the modern world, the bear is represented by conflicting images of the large predator and the soft, cuddly animal. The invention of the Teddy Bear as a toy happened in the beginning of the twentieth century when President Teddy Roosevelt refused to shoot a bear that had been trapped and tied to a tree by advanced scouts of his hunting party. Feeling it was too unsportsmanlike, he refused to shoot the bear and spared its life. The story led to a *Washington Post* political cartoon lightheartedly lampooning President Roosevelt, the "big-game hunter." Inspired by the cartoon, Morris Michtom, a candy shop owner and maker of stuffed toys, created a stuffed bear and named it Teddy in honor of President Roosevelt.

The more common interaction between people today in the Northwoods and the bear is during bear hunting season every September. Bear hunters often use dogs to tree the bears and we can occasionally hear hounds barking off in the distance at the cabin. The meat from bear is tasty, but quite dark and fatty. It is the skin as much as the meat that attracts hunters.

The black bear population has been a constant presence in this region for all of the thousands of years of human's shared history in this ecosystem, dating back to before the last glaciers receded from this area more than twelve thousand years ago. Even though they have a healthy and stable population in this ecosystem, they are an uncommon sighting. For the most part, black bears are solitary, active at night—though not strictly nocturnal—and generally wary of human activity. When they discover an easy food source such as garbage not properly disposed of around human habitation or an actual garbage dump, they will frequent that location in search of easy meals. The conflict this creates with the people sharing this ecosystem can result in the bear being trapped and relocated or more likely killed; once a bear finds such a food source, it will continually return, increasing the chance for a dangerous encounter with humans.

Though I have never seen a black bear in the woods around the cabin, I am aware of their presence from such clues as claw scratches in the white pine tree and seed-filled scat on the trail. The closest I have come to seeing a bear at the cabin is a nighttime photograph taken by the motion-activated trail camera set up to keep watch on the deer feeder. A small group of us were viewing the pictures taken the previous night, quickly clicking through the images: raccoon, our little white dog with brown ears, raccoon again, squirrel, raccoon yet again, fox, squirrel again, black bear...wait go back! Was that a bear? Sure enough, we were looking at the unmistakable silhouette of a black bear passing between the camera and the deer feeder. It only appeared in one photograph, meaning the bear did not stop to feed but just happened on through at the right place to have its image captured by the camera. It is a bit humbling to think that while we all slept inside during the night, a few yards from the cabin there was such a flurry of activity of small and large mammals.

The little blue pearls
Held up high for all to see
A toxin-filled bead
Looking almost good enough to eat
Connected by root to the next
And the next, and the next
This little plant owns the ground
Under my feet

Blue-Bead Lily

Clintonia borealis

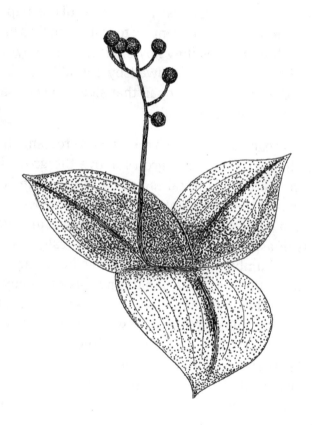

Vast patches of the blue-bead lily surround the cabin. The oblong and pointed leaves blend in with the tall fescue grass that dominates the ground cover. But the stalk, with its beaded fruit or flower atop, stands out tall in the grass. Though blue-bead is its common name, I was taught to recognize it by its genus name, *Clintonia.* It was named after DeWitt Clinton (1769–1828), governor of New York, presidential candidate, and the man who spearheaded the construction of the Erie Canal.

This is one of the first plants I learned to identify in the woods. I came to appreciate the consistency of the sprawling groundcover it provided. In the shade of the maples and aspens, the stalks reach from six to sixteen inches high and support diminutive yellow flowers from mid-May to early June. The flowers are followed by round, porcelain-like berries the size of a pinky nail that slowly form in a small bunch at the end of the stalk.

They spread easily through the use of a creeping rhizome, a root-like structure that grows above the ground away from the parent plant, takes root, and then sends up an extension of the first plant. Most of the blue-bead around the cabin could be parts of the same organism, much like stands of aspen trees might all be genetically one organism. I am humbled thinking of the fragility of my life, my one life, in this one time, inhabiting this one body, while this simple flower has found a means of achieving potential immortality. This might explain why the plant is common throughout the whole eastern half of the United States and Canada. Their strategy for immortality has not successfully protected them from habitat loss in other regions, however. The encroachment of cities and suburbs, and the conversion of woodlands into agricultural lands elsewhere have caused the blue-bead to be considered endangered or threatened in southern regions of the United States.

Before the flowers are pollinated and give way to the fruits that swell from the ovary at the base of the flower, the leaves are edible; with the taste of cucumbers, they are enjoyed by large mammals such as humans and deer. Once the fruit ripens, the only animal that can stomach the foul, mildly poisonous berry is the eastern chipmunk, *Tamius striatus*. Though Europeans that frequented the region as settlers, trappers, and voyageurs never found a medicinal use for the plant, the Ojibwe reportedly used the leaves to treat burns.

Years ago, as I landscaped my first house, trying to bring a piece of the cabin back to my home 200 miles to the south and west, my wife and I transplanted a few *Clintonia*. We dug them carefully, kept them moist as we transported them home, and even provided them with similar shade and soil. Despite our best efforts, we discovered, as many had before us, that this plant is notoriously difficult to cultivate. I should have known better than to try and replicate the uniqueness of the cabin. *Clintonia* belongs there, where it can be special. In my backyard, it would become common.

*[A]ny species that exempts itself from the rules of compe-
tition ends up destroying the community in order to support
its own expansion.*

—Daniel Quinn

Red Fox

Vulpes vulpes

At the top of the hill, very near the driveway, a red fox made a den for a couple of seasons. There was no mistaking the den as a red fox den: the tracks and the leftover bones and feathers from its prey gave it away.

It is amazing that these creatures are not more readily spotted. They are quite abundant, to the point that Wisconsin allows fox hunting with no bag limit. This is a testament to their general success as a species and, more particularly, to their elusiveness. Red foxes can be found all across the northern hemisphere, and now even in Australia as an introduced and invasive species. These animals are not large compared to their wolf cousins or even most domestic dogs, with a maximum shoulder height of twenty inches, and a total body length of up to thirty inches. These animals have been commonly trapped for their fur because of their abundance and wide-spread range, and because the fur is dense, soft, and relatively long.

Within the ecosystem of the Northwoods, the red fox is a skilled hunter. Their upright ears locate the rustling of such prey as a white-footed mouse to within one degree of direction. They usually approach their prey in silence and strike with incredible quickness. They hunt during any time of the day or night, but prefer the evening twilight when visibility is limited and their ears provide them an advantage over their prey. Though these animals have not evolved the same level of sophisticated pack dynamics as the timber wolf, they are social animals and work collaboratively to raise the kits. The young from previous years will often stay with the parents for a while beyond maturation. In so doing, they are then available to help care for the kits, and will delay their mating until they have become dominant enough in personality to venture off on their own and establish a new territory.

The range within which they hunt while living in the den is relatively small. Our local fox family probably does not stray far from the cabin. However, watching the den would not necessarily be an effective way to observe them. For the most part, the den is used only during the mating season and the early rearing of the five to six kits born in March, which is often before we open up the cabin for spring. By the end of June, the whole family is capable of venturing out into the forest to hunt in the evening or early morning. Once out of the den, the red fox prefers to bed down in protected locations throughout their range of 300 to 500 hundred acres and stay hidden from people.

Seeing the red fox is certainly a thrill, but I do not really mind that it's a rare occurrence. The deck is really stacked against me. The warning of the chickadee and the sound of my footfalls, no doubt, make the foxes aware of my presence long before I could actually see them. Despite my best efforts to tread lightly, I know they know better and will keep their distance or retreat into the safety of their den. This is the way it is in the woods. The majority of the life and the intricate interactions within this ecosystem proceed unnoticed until we cause a perturbation to the system. Maybe the chickadee is right to warn of my presence and the fox is wise in staying hidden. How can they know my intent is simply to watch and learn?

Let children walk with Nature, let them see the beautiful blendings and communions of death and life, their joyous inseparable unity, as taught in woods and meadows, plains and mountains and streams of our blessed star, and they will learn that death is stingless indeed, and as beautiful as life, and that the grave has no victory, for it never fights. All is divine harmony.

—John Muir

Smallmouth Bass

Micropterus dolomieu

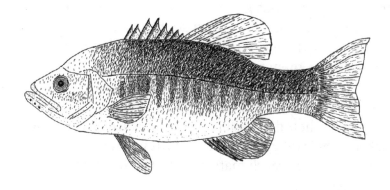

If I wanted to catch bass as a boy, there was one particular spot I could usually count on. It required crossing
the river in knee-deep rushing water. On the far bank, just
below the second set of rapids was a deep spot under the
cover of trees and near a glacial boulder four to five feet in
diameter. This was and is my favorite kind of fishing—wading in a quickly-moving stream, casting against the banks,
trees and other structures that provide cover for the fish.
No matter how many times it happens, or how old I get, I
do not get over the thrill of a bass snatching a lure, running
and then bursting out of the water as it tries to shake the
hook free. If the fish were not biting even at my favored

spot, I could avoid boredom by observing the birds—often belted kingfishers, diving for their meals—sharing the afternoon sun with me.

This river is good habitat for smallmouth bass, with a bottom that is a mixture of gravel suitable for nesting, and rocks from the size of my fist to glacial boulders to provide cover. I often found one in the shadowy spot below the largest boulder, as it was a perfect hiding spot for the male to retreat when not guarding the nest. The male bass is responsible for building a nest so the female has a place to lay her eggs. He then fertilizes and guards them for the few days it takes them to hatch. The offspring, called fry, sink to the bottom, hide for a few more days under the watchful eye of the male, and feed on microscopic crustaceans. As they grow, their diet widens to include insects and smaller fish and their range widens as well. It will take the fry three to four years to reach maturity and the strongest may live up to twelve years.

Many people who fish talk of "catch and release" like it is a virtue, as they put large, strong fish back into the water to reproduce and keep the population up. There have been multiple studies on the factors that increase the mortality rates of fish that are caught and then released, with results indicating that where the fish is hooked in its mouth and with what kind of hook are two of the most important factors. Artificial baits are less often swallowed by the fish and are therefore easier to remove without causing damage to the fish's esophagus. Also, hooks that are shaped more like a J, rather than hooks that are more circular in shape and curl back, are easier to remove. The longer it takes to remove the hook, the more time the fish spends out of water and therefore the more exhausted and stressed the fish becomes.

Exhaustion and damage from the hooks can leave the fish susceptible to disease, predation, and starvation, thereby increasing its mortality rate.

If handled quickly and properly with the proper equipment, mortality rates from catch and release are quite low. This practice still does not suit me, however, because it is at odds with my thinking rooted in deep ecology. I do not view the fish as a toy to be played with and then put back when done. In fact, this practice of catching and releasing strikes me as crueler than actually killing and eating the fish. Being caught and released is not a predatory behavior to which the fish has evolved, but being eaten is predation and is a part of life and part of their evolutionary history. When I have caught the amount of fish that I intend to eat, I prefer to simply stop fishing instead of continuing to fish just for the thrill of one more catch. To me, this better honors the life of the fish and my relationship with the fish as its potential predator.

When I'm done, I prefer to then spend my time watching and listening to the birds or feeling the cool water rush around my legs as I carefully pick my way over slippery rocks. The sound that the river makes can tell me its nature. If it is gurgling and speaking to me, I know that it is shallow enough to cross. But if it is silent, I should proceed with caution because the river is keeping secret what is in its depths. Observing which way the wind is pushing the trees can give me clues about the coming weather patterns. Sometimes the bigger thrill in the woods comes not from catching that granddaddy of a fish, but by putting the pole down and being quiet.

The world was not made for any one species.

—Daniel Quinn

Belted Kingfisher

Megaceryle alcyon

When fishing at the bass hole in the river near the cabin, I would always stop if I could watch the belted kingfisher. They are gifted hunters. They perch above a stream or river and watch for small fish, crustaceans, and amphibians. When one is spotted, they dive headlong into the water to catch it and then burst from the surface and fly back to their perch, whack their prey on the branch, then toss it in the air and swallow it whole.

Not far from the cabin, along the bank of the East Fork of the Chippewa River, there would have been no more than one nesting pair. A kingfisher pair will hunt up and down a territory that is about one thousand feet of shoreline. I have observed them many times while canoeing on other rivers. They always stay just ahead of me until reaching the end of their territory; then they loop back upstream and begin hunting again. I suspect they know that I don't pose a threat to them because they seem to go about their business while I fish, canoe, or just sit and watch.

There are some fishermen who see birds like the kingfisher and great blue heron as competitors for their game fish. I do not share this viewpoint. The way I see it, the birds need the food for their daily survival, and they were here first. I am a visitor, and should be a respectful guest in their habitat, though they have no obligation to be a gracious host to me.

For the most part, however, humans and kingfishers have a healthy relationship. Kingfishers nest in burrows they create along sandy banks, usually close to the water. They dig the burrow six to eight feet in depth, that slopes slightly upward, into a sandy bank, possibly to prevent flooding during high water. If the water rises above the entrance to the bank, an air pocket may be trapped in the end of the burrow. This pocket will keep the flood waters at bay and provide a temporary refuge for chicks. Modifying the river banks can destroy these nesting sites, but road cuts and bridge embankments can create them by exposing rocky and sandy banks.

Proximity to these birds, with their impressive hunting and their confidence despite my incursion into their space, is one of the reasons I enjoy being on or near the water, especially the streams and river near the cabin. I am always thankful for any time I get to share with this small but impressive hunter.

The sun sinks
Tangled in tree branches on the western shore
The crappies begin biting
When daylight fades into dusk
The canoe holds father and son
Filled with anticipation

Black Crappie

Proximos nigromaculatus

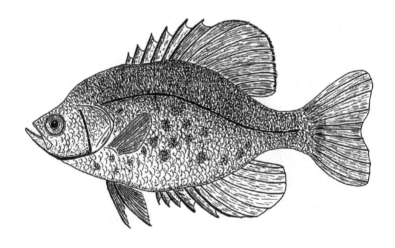

Thirty or so years ago, we could always count on catching crappies at sunset a few feet from the patch of wild rice on the northern bank of the lake. It was simple fishing—a bobber, a hook and a small minnow for bait. A crappie's mouth is described as a "paper mouth" because their lips and cheeks are thin, making it easy to yank the hook out and lose the fish before getting it into the boat. But when the crappies were feeding, it was hard *not* to catch fish, and I have fond memories of those evenings when Dad and I would paddle out to the spot we knew would produce fish. This is one of my early memories of connecting with the ecosystem of these woods—a dad and his young son quietly floating and fishing at sunset.

Crappie fishing has never been the same since those few abundant years during my childhood. I do not know what has changed, but back then, we could always count on a few crappies that were big enough to make a meal. Not so anymore. Either there has been a change in food supply for the crappie—small fish, crayfish, insects, tadpoles, and basically anything that will fit in their mouths—or there has been a change in the predators. Maybe there has been an increase in muskies, northern pike, great blue herons, or eagles on the lake. Or perhaps even the water temperature has changed. There has not been an increase in fishing pressure on the lake from people. It is lightly fished all year, so this is one change that cannot be pinned on the most dominant species in the area: humans. Whatever the reason, I do regret that I cannot call to my kids, the way that my dad called to me, "Hey, the sun is almost ready to set, let's go get a few crappies before they stop biting."

These are strong memories for me. My fondest crappie-fishing memory is from when I was no more than ten years old—before we built the cabin. Dad and I took his father crappie fishing. This was near the end of Grandpa's life, when he was battling lung cancer. Before his visit, we built a special seat for him to ride comfortably in the middle of the canoe. I felt a sense of responsibility beyond my years as I paddled in the front, with Dad in the stern and Grandpa the passenger in the middle. I was young when Grandpa passed, so I do not have many memories of him, but this one I carry close.

It used to sadden me that my daughters do not have a desire to fish, and that I did not provide them the same opportunities to take in the sunset while sitting in a quiet canoe as my dad did for me. However, I have become secure in the knowledge that this simply is not their way of connecting to the natural world. In the end, though, it is best they discover their own paths and own connections to the natural world, and to me. Forcing a replication of experiences to meet my own emotional needs does not necessarily meet theirs. So we have built our own memories as a family, and I suspect the ones that they will carry close, long into the future, are not the experiences we tried to manufacture but the seemingly insignificant moments my wife and I have long forgotten.

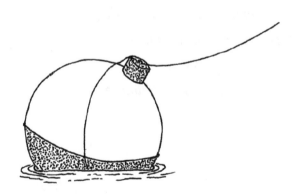

The merganser gliding
Below the water's surface
Searching, hunting and hiding
The merganser explodes
From the surface
Exhilarating, heart pounding

Common Merganser

Mergus merganser

When I was a boy, I liked to canoe the lake by myself. I liked the quiet, the solitude, and the independence. Mostly, I liked feeling grown up, managing the canoe alone. With my small amount of weight, the canoe was more like a leaf on the water than a carefully engineered watercraft, so I stayed in the bay at the west end of the lake, which never got much wind and was filled with wild rice and water lilies. In some places these plants were so thick that the canoe stopped between each stroke of the paddle.

I paddled as silently as possible, attempting a stealthy approach on frogs, turtles, a muskrat, or a beaver. If I closed my eyes and did not bang the paddle on the canoe's gunwales, the canoe could just as well have been made of birch bark, and I could be a voyageur or Ojibwe hunter.

Here is the scene: It is quiet. The canoe glides silently through an open spot in the vegetation. The slight breeze makes paddling easy. The water is glassy between the patches of lilies and wild rice surrounding the canoe. The sun is high and warm. No other boats or people are on the water. The only sound is the breeze. Suddenly, flapping wings explode from the water as a female merganser bursts out in front of the canoe. My heart pounds as the bird flies off and then glides onto the surface a safe distance away.

The merganser is a diving bird, plunging below the surface to hunt. It swims with grace and ease below the water's surface, using its serrated bill to catch small fish and frogs or tadpoles. Like all diving birds, it has solid bones. This advantage below the surface, however, requires considerable energy to escape the grasp of the water's surface tension and then stay aloft in the air. Like the common loon, the merganser cannot lift into flight without considerable effort. The merganser is an easy duck to recognize. It is fairly large—a little bigger than a mallard. The female has a distinctive orange head with tufted feathers off the back, as if it were wearing a warrior's headdress, offsetting a gray body.

An Ojibwe story about the merganser, or Shingebiss, teaches how the Ojibwe learned to adapt to the harsh, cold winters of the Great Lakes region. The story takes place in chemaywe'ya, the way back time. Shingebiss has a battle of wills with Kabibona'kan (winter) for survival. Shingebiss wins this battle and outlasts the spirit of winter. The battle ends when Kabibona'kan relents and pronounces, "I can neither freeze Shingebiss nor starve him; he is a very singular being. I will let him alone." Shingebiss teaches the importance of conservation, resourcefulness, and perseverance, lessons I learned as a young boy from such unstructured exploration of the world as paddling a canoe at the weedy end of a bay and being delighted by a bird sneaking up on me, instead of the other way around.

Life at the cabin has often provided these lessons. I remember getting stranded alone in the canoe, downwind from the cabin, and having to discover how to work with the wind and not against it. I also remember my brother digging our first sandpoint well, which involved pounding a four-inch galvanized pipe into the ground with a sledgehammer, one quarter of an inch at a time. My brother wielded that sledgehammer over and over to pound through sand, gravel, sandstone and glacial debris, for days on end. If the chosen spot happened upon a buried boulder, the options were to keep pounding and hope the point broke through, or to pick another spot and start over. At the elevation at which the cabin sits, a sandpoint well with a surface pump will only be able to pull water from about thirty feet down. At twenty-nine feet, there was still no water. Keep pounding. At twenty-nine feet, six inches...water.

Mom had one of her most harrowing cabin experiences during the digging of this well. After the sun had set, and the day's work was done, Dad and I were brushing our teeth in the kitchen, which was still under construction. The soon-to-be-finished well was situated in the open space under the cabin right below the kitchen. To make room for Chris's backswing when using the sledgehammer, Dad had cut away a section of the flooring. Each night the piece of flooring was placed over the opening. This night, however, it had not been properly placed and as Dad and I were at the sink, I stepped on the loose board, which tipped up like a trapdoor, and with a yelp and a crash, I disappeared into the hole. Dad turned toward the sound, but there was no Tim. I was just gone. Mom heard the crash and came running, her heart in her throat. Fortunately, I narrowly missed the pipe protruding from the ground. I was shaken but otherwise unharmed. Mom made sure that Dad properly secured the flooring each night after that until the well was finished.

We once watched dad slide off the roof with a circular saw in one hand, grasping for a handhold with the other, my mother scolding him all the way down for his carelessness. After falling the short distance from the edge of the roof to the ground—no more than ten feet or so—he picked himself up and got right back up on the roof. There was no one else to take over for him and finish the job, nor did the budget allow him to hire a contractor to do the tasks that at first appeared too daunting.

Many years later, to expand the cabin's living space and its seasonal usage, my dad, my brother, and I had many lessons in resourcefulness as we dug out the basement around the telephone poles on which the cabin stood. It required careful planning to support the cabin while we dug away the dirt anchoring the supporting poles and slid in new foundation walls constructed of treated wood. We eventually succeeded, after many discussions and plans drawn on napkins and scraps of paper, and the cabin even remained level throughout the entire process.

It's not only the men who have learned these lessons. Mom once spent an entire weekend mopping, scrubbing, and rescrubbing the floor on her hands and knees to clean up the mess left by one or more raccoons that broke into the cabin and had a party with a bottle of vegetable oil and a box of Bisquick. That is perseverance. For me then, Shingebiss is not a cheeky bird of the Northwoods, but an embodiment of the lessons I learned from my father, mother and brother over the years at the family cabin.

The merganser had more to teach me much later in life. As memorable as my first encounter with the merganser was, it was more thrilling for me thirty years later when the same thing happened to my daughter. Just as she was beginning a stroke, a merganser jumped from the water, right where she was placing her paddle. To have a close encounter with an animal is to know that animal and own that experience. To share an encounter with your child is a chance to pass on the best possible inheritance of all.

Everybody needs beauty as well as bread, places to play in and pray in where nature may heal and cheer and give strength to the body and soul alike.

—John Muir

Raccoon

Procyon lotor

Finding an animal cuter than a baby raccoon might be a challenge. Its cuteness has led many people to rescue (or maybe steal) abandoned baby raccoons, adopting them as pets. Unfortunately, for every bit of cuteness in a baby raccoon there are equal amounts of mischievousness and destructiveness in the adult. Whether breaking into the cabin and binging on vegetable oil and flour while the human occupants are away, rummaging through garbage, or leaving footprints all over the hood of a freshly washed car, the combination of intense curiosity, brazenness, intelligence, and nearly-opposable thumbs, means these masked creatures do not mix well (or mix *too* well, depending on the perspective) with human habitation.

The name raccoon possibly comes from the Algonquin word "arakun," which translates to, "he who scratches with his hands." A raccoon's front feet are more like hands than the feet of the other four-leggeds. Their thumbs are not truly opposable like primate hands, but they are nearly as dexterous. Coupling this physical trait with cat-like inquisitiveness makes them highly adaptable and successful around humans. Their adaptability has allowed raccoons to live successfully in nearly all of North and South America, and even in the Caribbean Islands. Twenty-two subspecies of raccoons have spread and evolved across the western hemisphere, with the Upper Mississippi River Valley subspecies inhabiting the Great Lakes region.

Raccoons are similar to the black bear in their adaptability to a variety of food sources and human habitation. They are truly omnivorous, eating almost anything: frogs, crayfish, clams, bird eggs, corn, berries, insects and nuts. City raccoons benefit from bird feeders, deer feeders, and garbage cans. To add to their cuteness, these masked bandits will "wash" their food by dipping the food into water before eating it. We humans are suckers for animals that emulate our behaviors. The traditional presumption is that they are washing it, but sometimes even near water they do not wash their food. It could be that some foods simply go down better when moist.

Such a wide diet can lead to some pretty portly creatures. In cities and towns where access to food is plentiful, adult raccoons can get quite large—up to forty pounds and three feet long. There is a purpose to the binging: by adding a one-inch-thick layer of fat between its muscle layer and skin, the raccoon stores the necessary fuel to keep a constant body temperature throughout the winter. Raccoons do not hibernate, though they may lay low in a den, a sheltered space under an uprooted tree, or in a hollow tree such as an elder basswood. By spring, adults will have burned up to fifty percent of their body weight to stay warm through the winter months. Many raccoons run out of fuel before spring and starve before warmth and snowmelt allow for adequate foraging.

In the spring, females will emerge from hiding, and soon after give birth to two to five young. Like kittens, raccoon kits are born helpless with closed eyes and need to stay in the protected den until able to forage for food with their mom. They will stay with her for twelve to fourteen months before heading out on their own.

Most of my raccoon encounters have not been in the woods around the cabin, where one would expect to see them, but instead have been near my home at the time in Northfield, MN. For several years, there was a large, mostly hollow, basswood tree in the backyard that housed a raccoon family. Each spring the mother would emerge from the tree with her young closely behind. There was no stealth in their nightly emergence. Crawling tail-first down the side of the tree, the mother and babies would work their way down and around the old tree, claws catching and scratching the rough bark all the way down.

At first, it was cute—unbelievably cute—and fun to watch. But then she started to cross some lines. The other safe place for the raccoons was under the garage, converted from an old carriage house. It had a wood floor with space underneath—perfect for raccoons. I did not mind them living there; but when I started to catch her lumbering away and down through a growing hole in the floor as I entered the garage, it seemed a little too close for comfort. Especially when I found so many footprints on the car hood that it looked like the mom was teaching her young son how to foxtrot before his first school dance.

The arms race escalated between me and mother raccoon (every bit of forty pounds) to keep her out of the garbage. Placing a cement block on top of the can or tight bungee cords clamping down the lid seemed only to invigorate her sense of resolve. Alerted by noise, I would look out the kitchen window to find her standing tall and rocking the plastic garbage dumpster back and forth until it tipped over. My presence was not a concern to her. Instead of scurrying away when I flicked the lights on, she simply gave me a look, as if to say, "What of it, old man?"

Then the line was obliterated when I heard a scratching and tapping on the porch screen door one summer night. I was up late, kept awake by the summer heat and humidity. I thought it was odd for someone to be coming to the door so late. Then I saw her, living up to her Ojibwe name, Arakun, standing tall and scratching at the screen door. I yelled and shooed her away. She gave me a backward glance as she lumbered off.

Our love–hate relationship came to an abrupt end during a violent thunderstorm. A crack of lightning jolted me out of bed one night as it struck the ash tree a few feet from the hollow basswood. The ash tree was dead and split down the middle, so we called a tree specialist in for a consult, However, it was the old basswood that he was most concerned about and amazed it had not fallen yet. So down came both trees, and I never saw the raccoon family again. I do not know what happened to the mother and her kits—whether the lightning got them or they moved on to another location. I do know that my garbage was left alone from then on and no late night callers came to my door.

Interactions with raccoons at the cabin are much more infrequent. We know they are there because we have had to clean up after their break-in and seal the garbage cans to prevent them from pillaging and spreading garbage around the cabin. But mostly we know they are there when we have the trail camera keeping watch. The most frequent visitor appears to be a very robust, well-fed family coming to raid the deer feeder. The foxes and deer prefer the early evening, but the raccoons are most often seen during the middle of the night. With great confidence (and girth) they waddle up and plop down right in the feeder and eat as much corn as possible. Clearly this is one "wild" animal that welcomes our settlement into these woods.

The tall lanky bird
Stands still as a statue
Waiting
Waiting
Waiting, until
A thrust of the beak
And snapping of jaws
Captures prey
Swimming below

Great Blue Heron

Ardea herodias

The great blue heron teaches lessons of patience and quiet confidence. As a totem for some indigenous peoples, the great blue heron brings messages of self-reliance, self-determination, and the ability to progress and evolve. Great blue herons are often underappreciated because they are a common bird, a bit ungainly, and rarely speak up for themselves. They do not produce many vocalizations, and before predators or humans can get too close, they lift off from their perches with a few easy flaps of their massive wings, and glide to a safe new location. Beyond their size—which, with a wing span of six to seven feet, is considerable—they are not physically remarkable. They are long and lanky. They have a tuft of feathers off the back of their heads that makes them look a bit disheveled. Their coloration is a simple blue-grey. They sometimes make a croaking noise, but more likely the only sound you will hear from these gentle giants is when they smack their top and lower bills together, making a clapping sound.

Having the wisdom of a great blue heron is to know oneself and how to follow one's own heart rather than the promptings of others. Those with the wisdom of the great blue heron will wait calmly while those around lose patience and raise a fuss. For this, I admire the heron. Considering myself a "late bloomer," I can relate to being underestimated as I think this bird often is.

Most often at the cabin we find great blue herons wading patiently at the edges of the water, amongst the tall wild rice plants, or stepping carefully with their long, spindly legs on and around the wet, slippery rocks that border the edge of the river flowing in and out of Barker Lake. These birds are generally solitary in their daily activities. When hunting, they are immensely patient—standing still for long stretches, waiting for the silhouette of a small fish or frog to pass under their gaze. With lightning speed, the heron plunges its beak into the water, snaring the prey, then tips its head back to swallow its meal whole. This is a learned skill. The elder herons have a much higher success rate at hunting than do the younger birds. It takes time to develop the necessary patience to wait for the right moment to strike.

Though these birds prefer wading in shallow water and striking at what swims silently below, they are not picky eaters. They are also quite adept at hunting on land and successful at catching small mammals, such as the white-footed mouse, and even insects.

When I have encountered great blue herons on the river, they have always kept their distance, appearing to be ignorant of my presence as I canoe quietly along. Before I can get too close, the heron easily lifts from the water, flapping its wings a few times to gain speed and altitude, clapping its bill, and then gliding to a new spot at the water's edge or in an overhanging tree. It will fly on ahead of me a hundred feet or so and then continue hunting until I get too close again, at which time it will repeat the pattern. When the heron tires of the game, it reverses course and flies back upstream behind me and continues with its day. I always feel like the annoying little brother to this quiet bird. It will put up with my pestering for a little while until it simply moves along and out of the reach of me and my canoe.

Great blue herons are not always hunting in solitude at water's edge with quiet confidence. When mating season arrives, they congregate in large groups, choose mates for the season, and build nests among a community of other mating pairs. This "heronry" is usually a collection of a hundred or more nests high up in isolated trees, difficult for land-dwelling mammals to reach. A main predator species for the eggs of great blue herons is the raccoon, which sneaks into their nests and steals the eggs or even the young hatchlings. Perhaps these normally solitary birds form these large nesting communities so that even when the parents are away feeding, there are always some adult herons around to ward off invaders.

One simple strategy they use is to vomit on the aggressor, although they are not always so passive–aggressive and can be quite violent if necessary. Their beaks can be formidable weapons, capable of piercing the skull of even the largest predators.

Great blue herons return to the same nesting community each breeding season, reusing a nest as long as possible. Like eagles, they continue to add to the nest until it reaches a diameter of up to four feet. This congregation of so many large birds in one location takes a toll on the local ecosystem, and in many ways they use up and trash a heronry faster than the local ecosystem can recover. Because of their diet, their waste is highly acidic, and it eventually kills the trees where they have built their nests. It is not uncommon to find dead fish, dropped by returning parents, scattered around the trees or hanging from branches. At the base of the trees will often be bodies of the one or two hatchlings that were pushed aside, and eventually out of the nest, by their larger, stronger siblings.

Perhaps there are lessons beyond patience and persistence to be learned from observing the great blue heron. We often assume that we are the only species that has not figured out how to live sustainably. We make the assumption that wild animals know not to inadvertently spoil their own habitats while humans cannot help but spoiling ours because we are no longer living in a "natural" way—that there is something wrong and unfixable with us; we have removed ourselves from nature. But of course, though we may perceive that we have removed ourselves from nature, this is not possible. Even living in the most concreted-over metropolis, we are not removed from nature. Even on a busy, city sidewalk, we are surrounded by and connected to life in a myriad of ways. There is a crucial difference though: we should know better. And it is also a matter of scale. When the health of the habitat in which the heronry is located gets depleted, the herons will eventually move on. Unfortunately, as the now dominant keystone species on the planet, there are very few places remaining that are not part of our own "heronry," and therefore very few places untouched by our attempts at making a habitat for ourselves. Certainly we humans have much to figure out when it comes to living sustainably, but we'd better do it quickly, because we don't have another location we can call home.

Let us permit nature to have her way. She understands her business better than we do.

—Michel de Montaigne

Wild Rice

Zizania aquatica

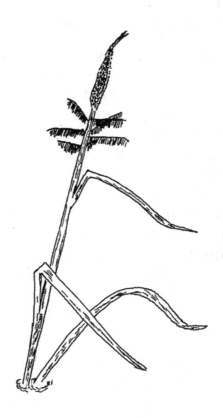

The tall, green, wild rice plants with small tassles on top usually fill the entire bay in front of the cabin from midsummer to late fall. They extend along the shoreline to the west and around the end of the lake and across to the northern shore. To the east from the dock, toward the main body of the lake, the wild rice fills a space more than two hundred yards long, thinning out as the bay opens to the larger lake. Years of boats going in and out, combined with diligent pulling of the plant, have resulted in a clear area around the dock and a channel to open water. But even where the wild rice has been eradicated, the remnants of their life cycle remain: twelve to eighteen inches of decaying organic muck, thick enough to pull off one's shoes.

During my childhood, I viewed wild rice as a weed that limited our swimming. At best, we could create a little alcove of open water amongst the plants. Occasionally we added sand and dredged out the brown, pungent, soupy mud from around the dock, reducing the muck depth to a manageable amount. We eventually reached a truce with the plants native to this bay and they yielded enough space for our dock and accompanying toys. As a boy, I did not appreciate what these plants meant to this ecosystem; I just wanted to play in the water. It certainly was an option to use harvesters and chemicals to eradicate and claim dominion over the aquatic system around the dock. Fortunately, twelve-year-old boys do not get to make such decisions, and the current compromise was struck—enough space for the boats, but no more.

Wild rice, though appearing to be perennial because it comes up in the same spot each year, is actually an annual. In the fall, seeds are released from the flower atop the plant. The dark brown, woody husks that give wild rice its characteristic texture and taste cause the seed to sink immediately to the bottom, thus keeping it from being eaten by waterfowl. About half of the seeds germinate each year. The rest remain dormant due to an imbalance in growth-regulatory hormones. The plants from the previous year die and sink to the bottom to fertilize the next year's crop, creating that shoe-sucking muck we try to avoid while swimming. Because of this life cycle, the wild rice does not spread quickly, but stays contained to one location until seeds are carried elsewhere by water current or animals.

I recall witnessing two men harvesting the wild rice one fall, poling a canoe through the weeds like the gondoliers in Venice. One man was standing in the back of the aluminum canoe while the other was using two sticks to bend the rice plants over the front of the canoe and then knock the rice grains from the fruiting body of the plant onto a tarp loosely stretched across the width of the canoe. He bent and knocked plants on one side of the canoe and then the other, ensuring a maximum harvest. They worked efficiently and quietly through the aquatic field of rice.

This plant, that has impeded my recreation, has long been a staple for the Ojibwe of this region and other tribes throughout North America. As the Ojibwe tell the story, Nanaboozhoo, a cultural hero, was introduced to wild rice by fortune and a duck. One evening, the story goes, Nanaboozhoo returned from hunting, but he had no game. As he approached his fire, a duck sat on the edge of the kettle of boiling water. The duck flew away and when Nanaboozhoo looked into the kettle he found wild rice, which he had never seen before, floating upon the water. He ate his supper from the kettle, and it was the best soup he had ever tasted. Later, he went in the direction the duck had gone and found a lake full of manoomin—wild rice. He saw all kinds of ducks, geese, mud hens, and all the other water birds eating the grain. After that, when Nanaboozhoo did not manage to kill a deer, he knew where to find food to eat.

Wild rice is more than just a basic food crop for the Ojibwe. It was their salvation. The Ojibwe people originally lived in the eastern part of North America. Prophets spoke of a great journey they would have to make westward across Turtle Island if they were to survive. This journey would be complete only when they reached a land where food grew abundantly in the water. The slow migration took many hundreds of years until the mid–1500s, when the Ojibwe found their special place in Northern Wisconsin and Minnesota. Looking out on the abundant rice in the lake, I know the prophets were right.

When fur trading began, the Ojibwe acted as middlemen between trappers and traders. The Ojibwe expanded their range throughout the great lakes region, directly into the wild rice habitat. This was especially true of the Lac Courte Oreilles band in north-central Wisconsin, who became quite industrious with the use and trade of wild rice. They maintained a semi-nomadic lifestyle, relying on hunting game for much of their subsistence, but also moved to their rice camps each August. Not only was the harvesting of the rice necessary for caching food for the coming winter, but also served as a ceremonial event with the annual congregation of families and relatives.

I look out at the wild rice now surrounding the dock, creating that consistent, familiar sea of green, and I cannot picture this bay as clear, open water. Sitting on the dock in the warmth of the midday sun is peaceful and quiet because of the protection provided by the wild rice; without it, I would feel exposed. The rice defines "our space" like a fence, making it more like a watery backyard than a lake. Birds are abundant, turtles and frogs quietly move among the stalks, taking no notice of us sitting on the dock. Without the omnipresent rice, it would be open water with limited accompanying wildlife.

Despite its dominant appearance in this ecosystem, wild rice is actually a delicate plant, highly susceptible to fluctuations in water height and pollution. Though the water is stained brown due to the local geology and vegetation, the presence and persistence of the wild rice indicates a nutrient-rich, well-balanced water system. I prefer to see the lake healthy instead of the rice receding and dying off, even if it would mean the bay would then be opened up for the recreation that I craved as a twelve-year-old boy.

First
One sings
Then another and another
Each adding his voice until
A chorus of song fills the nighttime air
Then one stops his drawn out "rummmm"
Then another and another
Each silencing his voice
Until just
One

Bullfrog

Rana catesbeiana

Today, the "rummmm" of bullfrogs is sporadic at best; a few here and a few there call throughout the day and into the evening. The chorus was different thirty years ago. Tadpoles and adults swam around the dock during the day, and then filled the night air with a rising and falling chorus loud enough to prevent those new to these woods a good night's sleep. The lake shallows teemed with frogs, providing endless amusement to me and my brother. We waded in the shoe-sucking muck and grabbed them with our bare hands. They were not hard to catch because of their abundance and because of their large size—up to ten inches in length from nose to toes. If held on their back with their abdomen rubbed, they slipped into a trance. Using a canoe paddle like a sixty-inch spatula, we scooped and flipped them, like green and pale yellow pancakes, legs flipping through the air and splashing back into the water like a high diver who's lost his bearing.

I now see that my relationship with the bullfrogs was somewhat abusive. Unfortunately for the "lower" animals, a boy's love of the natural world often involves this kind of exploration...and exploitation.

Just like the crappies, the bullfrogs have never been as abundant as during the summers of my youth. Maybe it is simply my perception, but I think not. More likely, both of these animals fulfill similar places in the food web of the lake ecosystem. Maybe their similar positioning means that whatever fate befalls one is also the reality for the other. What could cause such a decline? Bullfrogs are voracious predators, eating everything from small insects to small mammals. They are also prolific reproducers, laying up to twenty thousand eggs a year. It could be a natural cycle or a change in the balance of the ecosystem with less prey species available. Or maybe there are more predators now, as evidenced by the occasional frog missing the lower portion of a back limb. I imagine the bullfrog dodging and darting between wild rice stems, under and over lily pads, with the flash of a northern pike grabbing its leg. Multiply the pikes and you have an explanation for the smaller crappie population as well.

Frogs are susceptible to changes in the water quality, so the decline in population may be an indication of declining lake health. However, based on other environmental indicators of this region, such as the success of the relatively fragile wild rice, this does not appear to be the case. It could be that the population I remember so fondly was the anomaly and not the beginning of the long decline I perceive. Maybe the current levels represent an ecosystem in balance and the levels thirty years ago were unsustainable and wildly out of balance. I suspect that what I have witnessed over the years is the natural fluctuations of an ecosystem and the ability of that system to come to homeostasis.

Whatever the case, the chorus of calls building from one lonely frog to two, and then hundreds, each adding their drawn out "rummmm" to the night air, is how I prefer to perceive the norm for Northwoods bullfrogs. I miss having that large blanket of sound wrapped securely around my mind as I drift off to sleep. It is comforting to think that the chorus of the bullfrogs served the same purpose for me as a child as the cradleboard and dream catcher, with its eagle feather waving in the nighttime breeze, might have done for an Ojibwe infant in these same woods.

Above all we should, in the century since Darwin, have come to know that man, while captain of the adventuring ship, is hardly the sole object of its quest, and that his prior assumptions to this effect arose from the simple necessity of whistling in the dark.

—Aldo Leopold

Hairy Woodpecker

Picoides villosus

At first glance, distinguishing a hairy woodpecker from a downy woodpecker is difficult. The two species share almost identical markings, including the red spot on the back of the head on the males but not the females. Their behaviors are also nearly identical. To claim territory, the males of both species drum on hollow logs or sometimes, to the dismay of the homeowner, on a metal rain gutter early in the morning. The way to tell them apart is by size.

The hairy is slightly larger, with a difference in beak size as well. The hairy's beak is nearly equal in length to the depth of its head, whereas the downy's beak is much shorter. Both are typically found perched on the side of a tree, their tails forming the third leg of a sturdy tripod as they pick at bark, searching for insects.

Birds such as these prefer aspens or birches for food and nesting. When gathering food and building a home requires digging out the wood with a beak, softer wood is better. As the woods around the cabin transform from aspen-domi-nated to a hardwood forest, I suspect that the population of woodpeckers will decline.

I imagine it was only recently, a few million years ago at best, that these two species diverged from one another in their evolutionary history. It was probably a case of sym-patric speciation. The common ancestor of one of them adapted to a slightly different food source in the same hab-itat, thus allowing both to survive while occupying slightly different niches. Natural selection, in other words, worked out the "differences" of these two species and they now manage to share the same habitats.

It seems we humans could learn a lot from these little birds—lessons that apply to warring nations, political par-ties, classmates, siblings, and even cabin mates. When the entire extended family is at the cabin, we all have to find our "niches." And we do. Grandma is the meal-planner, caretaker, and professional worrier. Grandpa still needs to have a project in process, or in the wings, but he is always available to share with his grandchildren the lessons of the woods. He's happiest when he can combine the two. My older brother Chris, one of the quickest-witted people I know, always brings laughter and keeps us entertained. His dishwashing skills are admirable as well. His wife,

Angi, provides engineering expertise and once helped convince the construction crew—Dad, Chris and I—that two skylights were needed when we replaced the twenty-year-old roof. She also makes sure there is enough fruit for everyone at all times. Sarah, the oldest grandchild, was the leader of the other children, at least when they were all younger. Calvin, the oldest boy, brings us together in the living room for games. Carter is always willing to be Grandpa's apprentice and student. Linnea is the explorer, off in a kayak or riding the ATV on Darwin's Trail. Tyler, bearing the burden of always being the youngest, now fills the role of taskmaster and organizer of family games and activities. My wife, Tracy, brings the best of herself at the cabin. It is here that I see her laugh the most and be the most at ease. She teaches relaxation by example and, because Grandpa can't say no to his daughters-in-law, is the reason we now have a hot tub, which we all enjoy.

The joyful times at the cabin are when the entire family is gathered, filling the same habitat. Each brings his or her own gifts and perspective shared through late night conversations under the stars in the hot tub, around the fire, or gathered together in the main room playing a game. Chores are easier with more hands working together. Playing in the water or building a treehouse is more joyful when accompanied by many voices. The cabin is nice for quiet relaxation, but the true gift of this place is that it brings people together to create a common space to enjoy the peace and quiet within these woods. This is the gift it has given us all.

Behold, my brothers, the spring has come. The earth has received the embraces of the sun and we shall soon see the results of that love! Every seed is awakened and so has all animal life. It is through this mysterious power that we too have our being and we therefore yield to our neighbors, even our animal neighbors, the same right as ourselves to inhabit this land. My love of our native soil is wholly mystical.

—Chief Sitting Bull, Lakota

Downy Woodpecker

Picoides pubescens

I spot the downy early in the morning, flitting from branch to branch. I do not recognize that it is a woodpecker at first, mistaking him for a chickadee. They are almost the same size and have similar black and white markings. The exception is the red spot on the back of the head of the male downy, which this individual has. Like the chickadee, the downy spends the winter here in the Northwoods. They often mix in with the chickadees, foraging for similar foods and living in similar habitats, though their niche is slightly different, just as it is slightly different than their larger cousins, the hairy wood-pecker. I suppose the downy might prefer to remain with the sentinel chickadees to benefit from their warnings of approaching danger.

The downy is strictly an insect eater. He works his way around the tree trunk, poking and prodding until an insect is located, and then extracts it with his barbed tongue. I wonder if the chickadees benefit from the downy's foraging in any way—maybe they catch the insects the downy misses. If so, it would be a simple mutualistic connection between species. The downy benefits because the chickadee is always alert and ready to produce a warning when a potential predator is near, while the chickadee might be getting increased access to food. Maybe it is a relationship where the downy benefits and the chickadee is unaffected. This would be an example of a different kind of symbiosis called commensalism. Maybe even that is overthinking it, and they both simply share similar niches within the same preferred habitat.

I may not know for sure the exact nature of the rela-tionship between the chickadee and the downy, but what I do know is that I am aware of only a few of the seemingly endless connections between living things on this planet; and even then, my awareness is limited. For example, it is a good bet that most of the trees in this forest have millions of miles of fungal mycorrhizae strands growing around and into the cells of their roots.

This is an example of a mutualistic relationship. The fungi get easy access to the plant's carbohydrates that it has made through photosynthesis, and the increased sponge-like surface area created by the fungi strands increases the plant's ability to absorb water, an essential ingredient for photosynthesis. This is but one example of the many symbiotic relationships in these woods that often go unnoticed. And this is what amazes me the most as I wander through these woods. I cannot know and understand all of the connections. The endless possibilities of connections are too immense for me to realistically comprehend. This is when the woods become holy to me—and exploring them becomes spiritual.

Some people hear the voice of God in their dreams or through prayer or meditation. For me, God is truly in the details—the details found in the connections between the living things on the planet all working together to maintain the atmosphere and the soil. No, it is more than that. It includes all living things working together and in concert with all the nonliving things to maintain the living earth. The earth as a whole is truly alive. It has the ability, through the interactions of all the living and nonliving beings, to maintain itself. Scientists such as James Lovelock, who named this notion of the earth behaving like a living organism the Gaia Hypothesis, or Fritjof Capra, who has created a systems view of life, would argue that we have to understand all the connections to understand the individual. They prefer to think of the earth systemically, concentrating on the whole made up of the parts. Other scientists insist the whole can only be understood after understanding all the individual parts. I think both approaches are correct;

they both highlight different views of the same amazing processes of life.

I look up at a maple leaf waving back and forth in the breeze. I can almost hear the clicking of the electrons transporting across a membrane within the cell of the leaf, completing the process of capturing the sun's energy and beginning a chain reaction that results in glucose, the chemical fuel that drives all life on Earth. Glucose, this molecule that sustains and feeds our planet, is made from a combination of the most common of molecules. Carbon dioxide and water—these are the simple ingredients that fuel all life on the planet. The water in the leaf was absorbed with the aid of fungi that are intertwined around the plant's roots. These water molecules at one time might have been frozen on Mt. Everest or coursing through the veins of a prehistoric animal. The carbon dioxide taken in by the leaf could have been stored in the carbon sink of a Saudi Arabian oil field for millions of years. The plant then releases oxygen into the atmosphere to our benefit, as we exchange the excess carbon dioxide in our lungs for the oxygen released into the atmosphere by the plants—yet another connection.

While I walk in these woods, somewhere in the Amazon a butterfly is sucking the nitrogen out of the droppings of an ant bird that is following a horde of army ants that are attacking insects. Ants feed birds, which feed the butterfly—a butterfly which then breathes out carbon dioxide, which is then absorbed into the leaf of an Amazon tree, where the carbon dioxide molecules are combined with water molecules by the plant, using energy it absorbed from photons from the sun, to make glucose. This glucose is digested by the insects that eat the leaves and are then pursued by the ants. More connections. The tree releases oxygen when doing photosynthesis to make the glucose and the winds carry the oxygen far away—perhaps to a maple forest in Northern Wisconsin to be breathed in by a small bird, pecking at the side of a tree in search of an insect, which is being observed by a middle-aged man marveling at the wonder of it all.

Days shorten and nights cool
Sky is high and water low
Summer ending fall approaching
The cabin will soon be closed

The geese organize and take flight
Cutting across yellow, orange
And the ephemeral band of green
Into the black of night

Canada Goose

Branta canadensis

It is fall and cabin season is coming to a close. Days shorten from their peak of nearly seventeen hours down to twelve on the fall equinox and shorter still to come in the winter. The mornings are increasingly cool. Yellow and orange pigmentation are revealed in the maple leaves as the plant lets the green chlorophyll molecules fade away, saving energy in anticipation of a cold, low-sunlight season.

Chlorophyll is a complex molecule, requiring a significant investment by the plant to assemble. Absorbing the sun's light energy comes at the cost of the chlorophyll, which is decayed by the same energy it is designed to absorb. So as the days shorten, the trees know through millennia of adaptation and wisdom transmitted genetically across the generations that it is best to let go and rest up for the next season. Soon the leaves will fall and sunlight will once again reach the forest floor, filtered only by the naked skeletons of the trees.

This transition is also marked by honking Canada geese flying overhead in their characteristic V formation as they head south for the winter. The lead bird breaks through the wind, increasing the flying efficiency of the ones that follow. When the lead bird gets tired, another takes its place. How the geese figured out this system baffles me. Long before Nascar drivers and Tour de France riders discovered the art of drafting, these birds mastered it. The result is an amazingly complex social behavior hardwired into their DNA. Does each goose organize this way for its own benefit, or does it have a communal goal in mind? Maybe the intention does not matter. The advantageous practice evolved and has been passed on from generation to generation, benefiting the individual and the community at the same time. I suppose the needs of the many and the one do not have to be mutually exclusive.

More spectacular to me than the geese, however, is the band of green across the sky. This magnificent green band of light appears at dusk. It is a short-lived color in the evening sky, separating the dark blues above from the orange glow left behind by the setting sun. Lasting only a few minutes as day gives way to night, it is my favorite time at the end of a clear, autumn day, the kind that exemplifies a "beautiful day"—all sun, a comfortable temperature, and a slight breeze carrying that delicious fall smell. When the breeze recedes, the warmth of the high sun feels like a warm blanket. The pale blue of the sky seems to extend for eternity on these days.

It has been more than thirty years since my mom and dad first found this place. During that time the cabin has grown, with new out-buildings for storage, additional space for sleeping, swings, treehouses, boats and other modern toys for recreation, and trails for exploration and reflection. Children, grandchildren, grandparents, parents and the occasional visitor discover their own lessons and beauties of the cabin—the relationships with the woods, one another, and ourselves. Though a significant time in the life of our family, these years are but a moment in the longer history of people within the woods of this evolving Northern Wisconsin ecosystem. Beginning with the recession of glaciers around fifteen thousand years ago, through all the occupants that have come before us and all those that will follow, our presence is as ephemeral as that green band in the evening twilight. I pause and watch the geese silhouetted against this momentary coloration in the sky. The green fades as the stars and the planet Venus appear at the end of another fall day in the Northwoods.

We need myths that will help us to identify with all our fellow-beings, not simply with those who belong to our ethnic, national or ideological tribe.

—Karen Armstrong

The Night Sky

Noctis caelum

Nighttime at the cabin means stars. Since there is no light pollution, it is pitch black on moonless nights. Being at the cabin with friends on such a night, I have learned that most people have never experienced complete darkness. In fact, when asked what they would see in a room with no light, most children respond that after a few minutes their eyes would adjust and then they would be able to see at least some shapes and larger objects in the room. However, if there is no light, there is no seeing. But of course, seeing is not the only way to know something.

When the moon is up, especially a full moon, enough sunlight is reflected down upon us to almost see color. But it is the darkness of moonless nights that I prefer, when we can sit in the hot tub or on the dock, or even go out in the pontoon boat and drift silently in the darkness. We look up at the stars and see the familiar constellations, the band of stars creating the Milky Way galaxy, and sometimes the planets—usually Mars and Jupiter. The stars are reflected across the water when it is perfectly calm and still.

I know the stars in the constellations taught to me by my father. These are the constellations connected to stories from deep in western culture's history. Probably the most recognizable of these is Orion the hunter. When I taught astronomy to high school students, I had them make a three-dimensional model of a constellation such as Orion. The stars were represented by beads on threads hanging in relative position to each other. The end result was a model that looked like a mobile that would hang above a baby's crib. Viewed from the vantage point of Earth, the grouping of stars was recognizable as Orion. However, if you rotated the constellation mobile, the constellation was no longer recognizable because the beads were hung in relative distance from each other and from Earth. The stars that appear to be close to each other from a frontal view were actually separated by a great distance when viewed from the "side." Taken to scale, this distance would represent light years of separation. If Orion could be viewed from a different vantage point, that group of stars would look nothing like our bow-wielding hunter; the stars in Orion's sword in fact are nowhere near each other. This is the case with all of the prominent constellations we see in the northern sky: the Big and Little Dipper (both part of bigger constellations representing Big Bear and Little Bear), Cassiopeia, Cygnus the Swan, and Taurus the Bull. The night sky reminds me that it really is all a matter of perspective—and not just the western perspective.

Polaris was equally important to the indigenous peoples of North America as it was to the Europeans, and probably to all cultures in the northern hemisphere. They too noticed that the North Star is the only heavenly body that is stationary throughout the night and even throughout the year. It stays in a fixed position above the planet's North Pole, or within two degrees at least, which is close enough to be useful for navigation.

We can see the North Star, as well as the rest of the circumpolar constellations, from the deck of the cabin through a clearing in the trees and from the north-facing dock. Viewed from this vantage point, the most prominent are the Big Dipper, Little Dipper and Cassiopeia. The last two stars in the cup of the Big Dipper can be used to find Polaris, which is not the brightest star in the sky. If you were to draw a line through the last two stars of the cup and, with your arm outstretched all the way, extend the line three fists widths, you would run into Polaris, which is also the first star in the handle of the Little Dipper. Opposite Big Bear on the other side of Polaris is Cassiopeia, the queen.

The Milky Way is a band of brightness that extends from Cassiopeia in the north to Scorpio in the south, appearing as a milky-colored path across the sky. Through binoculars aimed at the Milky Way, the sky looks completely filled with stars. With the unaided eye, about three thousand stars are visible. When looking up at the band of stars that are the Milky Way, we are actually looking toward the middle of our galaxy, as we are positioned on an outer arm of the spiral galaxy. To some indigenous peoples, the Milky Way is the path followed by souls into the other world. For others, the portal to the other side of the celestial sphere is through Big Bear's "cup."

The most common story of the Big Dipper and Little Dipper, or Ursa Major and Ursa Minor, comes from a Greek myth that if told to a modern day psychiatrist might cause him or her to sit up straight and take prodigious notes. The story is that Callisto, the beautiful mother of Arcus, was washing clothes in a creek when Zeus, the king of the gods, came along and helped her with her washing. They spent the next few days together and Zeus showered her with gifts. This angered Hera, Zeus' fiancée, who in her jealous anger turned Callisto into a bear. This left Arcus without a mother, but he grew up to become a great hunter. Once, while hunting in the woods, Arcus came across a great bear, who unbeknownst to him was Callisto. Zeus was also in the woods and tried unsuccessfully to convince Arcus of the true identity of the great bear. In desperation, before Arcus could kill his own mother, Zeus turned him into a small bear, who then finally recognized Callisto as his mother and embraced her. Hera angrily sought out the bears, but before Hera could harm them, Zeus grabbed both bears by their tails and flung them into safety in the northern sky. The tails of these bears are longer than those of their earthbound cousins because they were stretched out by Zeus' throw.

The Ojibwe also have stories about the formation of the stars, including one about a boy named Little Bear, whose father, Big Bear, lived in the sky. Little Bear asked his grandfather about the two moons in the sky, wondering if anyone lived on the moons, and why they had two moons when one should be enough. Grandfather explained that once there were two worlds that shared our sun. They lived in harmony but as time passed, evil took over the other world and the good people migrated to ours. The Creator took pity on us and sent the evil people far away from the sun and back to their world. He then took away their moon so as to leave them in darkness. The Creator told our people that one day a child would come who would have the power to make a place in the sky for all. After his task on Earth was finished, the child would be given a special place in the heavens beside his father, Big Bear. Grandfather told Little Bear that his destiny was coming, as seen by Little Bear in a dream.

One day Little Bear said goodbye to his grandfather, took his bow and arrow, and climbed the highest hill he could find. He pulled back his bow as far as he could and shot his arrow into the center of the brightest moon. The moon exploded and shattered, spreading millions of stars throughout the sky. Little Bear, realizing that he had seen his grandfather for the last time, said goodbye to the old man, and with his heart beating faster, traveled up to the sky to forever join his father, Big Bear. Now Big Bear and Little Bear travel together every night.

As I sit on the dock under these familiar constellations, as an average son with his average father, on this average lake, on our average planet, traveling around an average star that is one of billions of other average stars, in an outer arm of our average spiral galaxy—one of billions of galaxies, containing billions of stars—I am humbled. Yet as easy as it would be to feel insignificant and alone under this vast night sky, I instead feel rooted to this place, connected to the life in these woods, and therefore part of something miraculous. And so, I conclude with this final thought:

Life feels itself
The warm mother earth
A continuous rebirth

Life feels itself
The cold rain drips down
Soaks into the ground

Life feels itself
Through all time and space
Offering Gaia's grace

Life feels itself
On this blue-green ball
Connecting one to all

Life feels itself
In the warm summer sun
Until the day is done

Life feels itself
The green leaf breathes deep
All our souls to keep

Life feels itself
With each recycling breath
Raising life from death

Life feels itself
Ancient ancestors to me
Ancient ancestors to me.

Acknowledgments

Completion of this project has been a long time coming and it would not have been possible without the assistance of many colleagues, friends and family. The first illustration and poem, large-leafed trillium, was completed while team-teaching a course titled Nature Through the Arts, with artist and colleague Dominic Fucci. We were both employed at the Northfield School of Arts and Technology Charter School and we were leading a group of students in exploring the confluence of art and the natural world. To lead by example, we felt it was important to add to the working portfolio of the class. Little did I know that this effort would be the beginning of a ten-year project. I would like to thank Dominic and our students for their willingness to put up with a science teacher exploring his creative soul as it worked its way out from under the lab coat.

After the project began to take shape, it was Scott Grave and T McKinley who were the first readers and reviewers of the book. Their advice and encouragement was crucial to providing the confidence necessary to make this book real. I urge you to find T's first book, *The Boy in the Ivy*. It's an impressive piece of work. It was also T, near the end of the process, who continued to challenge me to dig a little deeper and explore more than just the "nature stuff" and tell more of "my story". Thanks, I think. Thanks also go to my wife's parents, Tom and Carol Hasek, for their assistance and advice along the way in fleshing out the ideas of the essays. My colleague, Porter Coggins at Bemidji State University, also requires mentioning for his continued support and advice as well. The first round of expert and professional editing was provided by Michael Lotti, from Lotti Writing Services, without which this project would not have been possible. This feedback was crucial to the process and invaluable to the development of the book. He did not have the final word in editing, though, as more essays were added, existing essays morphed as the narrative evolved, and the sequence of the essays changed as well. The final edit was completed by my wife, Tracy, who, though she may not like doing it, is a talented editor. As much as this project was a labor of love for me, it was an act of devotion for her, and I am forever thankful and grateful. Most importantly, the marriage survived. While having your spouse edit your writing is certainly a lesson in humility, I suspect editing your spouse's work is a lesson in patience and dedication.

Daniel Rice, of Riverfeet Press, deserves mention as well. Throughout the final stages of the publication process he was always positive, supportive and responsive to my ideas and opinions—no matter how many times I said, "What if we tried..." His keen eye and expert skills were responsible for moving this project from manuscript to a tactile book.

Returning back to the beginning, it was watching the five grandchildren at the cabin that inspired me to dig in, find the stories to tell, and turn this simple curiosity and exploration of the natural history of the Northwoods into a project with a purpose. And lastly, there are not enough words to express my gratitude to Tom and Dorothy Goodwin for making the decision to buy the property, build the cabin, and then continue to make the cabin a focal-point for family gatherings. There must not be enough words, because after some forty thousand, I still do not feel like it is properly expressed—but I hope this is enough.

After teaching secondary science for 20 years, Tim Goodwin is now in the Department of Professional Education at Bemidji State University. With a M.A. and Doctorate in Education from Hamline University, and a Bachelor's degree in Biology from St. Olaf College, Dr. Goodwin's research involves work in environmental education, ecological literacy and ecological identity. Goodwin has also written *Ecological Identity: Finding Your Place in a Biological World* (Riverfeet Press, 2017) and *Consider, Construct, Confirm: A New Framework for Teaching and Learning* (Kendall Hunt, 2020). In addition to teaching, writing and illustrating about the natural world, he is also a musician.

Find Dr. Goodwin's blog, music and other information at:

www.timothygoodwin.net.

Printed in the U.S.A.

www.riverfeetpress.com

CPSIA information can be obtained
at www.ICGtesting.com
Printed in the USA
LVHW030349180321
681768LV00006B/1297

9 781736 089422